# GIVE ME LIBERTY!
## An American History

### INSTRUCTOR'S MANUAL
### AND TEST BANK

VOLUME TWO

# ERIC FONER

# GIVE ME LIBERTY!
## An American History

# INSTRUCTOR'S MANUAL
# AND TEST BANK
## BY

# Valerie Adams
EMBRY-RIDDLE AERONAUTICAL UNIVERSITY

## VOLUME TWO

W · W · NORTON & COMPANY · NEW YORK · LONDON

ISBN 0-393-92552-8 (pbk.)

W. W. Norton & Company, Inc., 500 Fifth Avenue, New York, N.Y. 10110
www.wwnorton.com

W. W. Norton & Company Ltd., Castle House, 75/76 Wells Street, London W1T 3QT

1 2 3 4 5 6 7 8 9 0

# CONTENTS

# PREFACE

This *Instructor's Manual and Test Bank* accompanies *Give Me Liberty! An American History* by Eric Foner. A groundbreaking textbook, its focus on freedom is a unifying theme that has much relevance for students today. The *Instructor's Manual and Test Bank* highlights that theme throughout, in an effort to help the instructor emphasize it in lectures and discussions.

This manual also helps instructors assess student mastery of the basic American history narrative. In today's political and diplomatic climate, public discussion often turns on issues of "freedom" and "liberty". The war on terrorism, which is being waged in part to protect American freedom, simultaneously impinges upon American freedom. Our conceptions of freedom have evolved over the centuries and Foner's text reminds us of our national struggle to broaden the definition so as not to exclude anyone. Freedom might entail property ownership, economic freedom, the freedom to speak out against the government, or the freedom to sit anywhere on a public bus. By tracing the constantly changing meanings of freedom in the context of an introductory American history, Foner has given us a textbook that is both timely and superbly written for the survey course. It is my hope that even seasoned veterans of the survey course find that the companion *Instructor's Manual and Test Bank* is useful for integrating the material in *Give Me Liberty!* into their current class curriculum.

The *Instructor's Manual* comprises the following elements for each chapter of the text: A chapter summary that offers a quick overview of the major themes and the topic of the *Voices of Freedom* primary-source insert. A detailed chapter outline follows, which can be used for lecture notes or PowerPoint presentations. The discussion of supplemental Web/visual material provides at least one video suggestion in addition to recommended Web sites that highlight the liberty theme. The discussions of supplemental print materials emphasize the most recent historical scholarship in monographs and journal articles. A series of classroom discussion questions concludes the *Instructor's Manual* portion.

The *Test Bank* includes some 2,000 matching, multiple-choice, true/false, short answer, and essay questions that assess student mastery of basic names, dates, and events. This volume also offers critical thinking, discussion, and essay questions that attempt to link various chapters and recurring themes. The intention of the volume is to balance pure memorization questions with application and critical thought questions, thereby providing a variety of exam questions to suit different needs and testing styles. For high-school teachers, the *Test Bank* complies with the Advance Placement format by offering five choices with each multiple-choice question.

This volume aims to help instructors new to the survey course with extensive chapter outlines, classroom discussion questions, and more than seventy test questions for each chapter. However, it also offers something for the experienced instructor by highlighting the freedom theme in the chapter summary, discussion, and essay questions and by suggesting new scholarship and Web sites.

My deepest appreciation and gratitude is extended to Steve Forman, senior editor at W. W. Norton, whose talent and vision made this volume infinitely stronger. I am also indebted to Sarah England at W. W. Norton for her patience and guidance through this project. Finally, I thank both Eric Foner and W. W. Norton for publishing a textbook that I hope inspires other instructors as it has inspired me and amplified my passion for the American history survey course.

Valerie Adams

**CHAPTER 15**

# "What Is Freedom?":
# Reconstruction, 1865–1877

This chapter concentrates on the history of Reconstruction. Opening with an explanation of Special Field Order 15 from General Sherman that set aside "40 acres and a mule" for the freedmen, the chapter explores what freedom meant to blacks and how white American society responded to emancipation. The meanings of freedom for blacks were many, and they relished the opportunity to express their liberation from slavery. Land ownership became a contentious issue as blacks were ultimately denied free access to land. Highlighting this controversy is *Voices of Freedom,* which features a petition from freedmen to Johnson in regards to land. Likewise, due to the devastation caused by the Civil War, many white farmers newly faced poverty as tenant farmers and sharecroppers. The politics of Reconstruction is explored next, viewing Lincoln's Ten-Percent Plan as moderate, Andrew Johnson's plan as too lenient, and the Radical Republicans' plan as groundbreaking. With Johnson's many presidential pardons to ex-Confederates and the South's implementation of Black Codes, the Republicans in Congress fought back with the Civil Rights Act of 1866, the Fourteenth Amendment, and the Military Reconstruction Act. Johnson resisted and was impeached by the House, but avoided being removed from office by the Senate. The Fifteenth Amendment finished the Radical Republicans' Reconstruction agenda, but split the feminist movement due to its failure to give the vote to women. The chapter then looks at how Reconstruction shaped southern politics as blacks held over 2,000 public offices. The white southerners, however, felt threatened by black suffrage and the Ku Klux Klan began a campaign of terror and violence. After the Klan was abolished through the efforts of President Grant, the South took matters into its own hands and began to "redeem" itself from perceived corruption, misgovernment, and northern and black control. Reconstruction ended in 1877, after a compromise was met between the Republicans and Democrats on the 1876 presidential election.

# CHAPTER OUTLINE

I. "Sherman Land"

II. The Meaning of Freedom
  A. Blacks and the Meaning of Freedom
    1. African-Americans' understanding of freedom was shaped by their experience as slaves and observation of the free society around them
    2. Blacks relished the opportunity to demonstrate their liberation from the regulations, significant and trivial, associated with slavery
  B. The Black Family in Freedom
    1. The family was central to the post-emancipation black community
    2. Freedom subtly altered relationships within the family
      a. Black women withdrew to their private sphere
  C. Church and School
    1. The rise of the independent black church, with Methodists and Baptists commanding the largest followings, redrew the religious map of the South
      a. Black ministers came to play a major role in politics
    2. Blacks of all ages flocked to the schools established by northern missionary societies, the Freedmen's Bureau, and groups of ex-slaves themselves
  D. Political Freedom
    1. The right to vote inevitably became central to the former slaves' desire for empowerment and equality
      a. Being denied suffrage meant "the stigma of inferiority"
    2. To demonstrate their patriotism, blacks throughout the South organized July 4th celebrations
  E. Land, Labor, and Freedom
    1. Former slaves' ideas of freedom were directly related to land ownership
      a. Many former slaves insisted that through their unpaid labor, they had acquired a right to the land
  F. Masters without Slaves
    1. The South's defeat was complete and demoralizing
      a. Planter families faced profound changes
    2. Most planters defined black freedom in the narrowest manner
      a. Freedom was defined as a privilege, not a right
  G. The Free Labor Vision
    1. The victorious Republican North tired to implement its own vision of freedom
      a. Free labor
    2. The Freedmen's Bureau was to establish a working free-labor system

  H. The Freedmen's Bureau
   1. The task of the Bureau was daunting
   2. The Bureau's achievements in some areas, notably education and health care, were striking
  I. Land and Labor
   1. Blacks wanted land of their own, not jobs on plantations
   2. President Andrew Johnson ordered nearly all land in federal hands returned to its former owners
   3. Because no land distribution took place, the vast majority of rural freed people remained poor and without property during Reconstruction
  J. Toward a New South
   1. Sharecropping came to dominate the cotton South and much of the tobacco belt
   2. Sharecropping initially arose as a compromise between blacks' desire for land and planters' for labor discipline
  K. The White Farmer
   1. Aftermath of the war hurt small white farmers
    a. Crop lien
   2. Both black and white farmers found themselves caught in the sharecropping and crop lien systems
    a. Every census from 1880 to 1940 counted more white than black sharecroppers
  L. The Urban South
   1. Southern cities experienced remarkable growth after the Civil War
    a. Rise of a new middle class

III. The Making of Radical Reconstruction
  A. Andrew Johnson
   1. Johnson identified himself as the champion of the "honest yeomen" and a foe of large planters
   2. Johnson lacked Lincoln's political skills and keen sense of public opinion
   3. Johnson believed that African-Americans had no role to play in Reconstruction
  B. The Failure of Presidential Reconstruction
   1. Johnson's plan for Reconstruction offered pardons to the white southern elite
   2. Johnson's plan allowed the new state governments a free hand in managing local affairs
  C. The Black Codes
   1. Southern governments began passing new laws that restricted the freedom of blacks
   2. These new laws violated free-labor principles and called forth a vigorous response from the Republican North

D. The Radical Republicans
  1. Radical Republicans called for the dissolution of Johnson's state governments and new ones established without "rebels" in power that gave blacks the right to vote
  2. The Radicals fully embraced the expanded powers of the federal government born of the Civil War
    a. Charles Sumner
    b. Thaddeus Stevens
  3. Thaddeus Stevens's most cherished aim was to confiscate the land of disloyal planters and divide it among former slaves and northern migrants to the South
    a. His plan was too radical
E. The Origins of Civil Rights
  1. Most Republicans were moderates, not radicals
  2. Senator Lyman Trumbull of Illinois proposed two bills to modify Johnson's policy
    a. Extend the life of the Freedmen's Bureau
    b. Civil Rights Bill
  3. Johnson vetoed both bills
  4. Congress passed the Civil Rights Bill over his veto
F. The Fourteenth Amendment
  1. It placed in the Constitution the principle of citizenship for all persons born in the United States, and empowered the federal government to protect the rights of all Americans
    a. It did not provide for black suffrage
  2. The Fourteenth Amendment produced an intense division between the parties
G. The Reconstruction Act
  1. Johnson campaigned against the Fourteenth Amendment in the 1866 mid-term elections
  2. In March 1867, over Johnson's veto, Congress adopted the Reconstruction Act
H. Impeachment and the Election of Grant
  1. To demonstrate his dislike for the Tenure of Office Act, Johnson removed the secretary of war from office in 1868
  2. Johnson was impeached and the Senate fell one vote short to remove him from office
  3. Ulysses S. Grant won the 1868 presidential election
I. The Fifteenth Amendment
  1. Congress approved the Fifteenth Amendment in 1869
  2. Provided for black suffrage
    a. Had many loopholes
    b. Did not extend suffrage to women

J. The "Great Constitutional Revolution"
   1. The laws and amendments of Reconstruction reflected the intersection of two products of the Civil War era—a newly empowered national state and the idea of a national citizenry enjoying equality before the law
   2. Before the Civil War, American citizenship had been closely linked to race
      a. Naturalization Act of 1790
      b. *Dred Scott* decision of 1857
   3. The new amendments also transformed the relationship between the federal government and the states
K. The New Boundaries of Freedom
   1. That the United States was a "white man's government" had been a widespread belief before the Civil War
   2. Reconstruction Republicans' belief in universal rights also had its limits
      a. Asians still excluded from citizenship
L. The Rights of Women
   1. The destruction of slavery led feminists to search for ways to make the promise of free labor real for women
   2. Other feminists debated how to achieve "liberty for married women"
M. Feminists and Radicals
   1. Talk of woman suffrage and redesigning marriage found few sympathetic male listeners
   2. Feminists were divided over their support for the Fifteenth Amendment
      a. National Women Suffrage Association
      b. American Woman Suffrage Association
   3. Despite their limitations, the Fourteenth and Fifteenth Amendments and the Reconstruction Act of 1867 marked a radical departure in American and world history

IV. Radical Reconstruction in the South
   A. "The Tocsin of Freedom"
      1. Among the former slaves, the passage of the Reconstruction Act inspired an outburst of political organization
      2. These gatherings inspired direct action to remedy long-standing grievances
      3. The Union League aided blacks in the public sphere
      4. By 1870 the Union had been restored and southern states held Republican majorities
   B. The Black Officeholder
      1. Two thousand African-Americans occupied public offices during Reconstruction
         a. Fourteen elected to the House of Representatives
         b. Two elected to the Senate

    2. The presence of black officeholders and their white allies made a real difference in southern life

    3. Robert Smalls of South Carolina

  C. Carpetbaggers and Scalawags

    1. Carpetbaggers were northerners who often held political office in the South

    2. Scalawags were white southern Republicans

  D. Southern Republicans in Power

    1. Established the South's first state-supported public schools

    2. The new governments also pioneered in civil rights legislation

    3. Republican governments also took steps to strengthen the position of rural laborers and promote the South's economic recovery

    4. Every state during Reconstruction helped to finance railroad construction

V. The Overthrow of Reconstruction

  A. Reconstruction's Opponents

    1. Corruption did exist during Reconstruction, but it was confined to no race, region, or party

    2. Opponents could not accept the idea of former slaves voting, holding office, and enjoying equality before the law

  B. "A Reign of Terror"

    1. Secret societies sprang up in the South with the aim of preventing blacks from voting and destroying the organization of the Republican Party

    2. Ku Klux Klan organized in 1866

      a. It launched what one victim called a "reign of terror" against Republican leaders, black and white

  C. The Challenge of Enforcement

    1. Congress and President Grant put an end to the Ku Klux Klan by 1872

  D. The Liberal Republicans

    1. The North's commitment to Reconstruction waned during the 1870s

    2. Some Republicans formed a new party called the Liberal Republicans

      a. Horace Greeley

    3. Liberal Republicans believed that power in the South should be returned to the region's "natural leaders"

  E. The North's Retreat

    1. The Liberal attack on Reconstruction contributed to a resurgence of racism in the North

    2. The 1873 depression also distracted the North from Reconstruction

    3. The Supreme Court whittled away at the guarantees of black rights Congress had adopted

    F. The Triumph of the Redeemers
       1. Redeemers claimed to have "redeemed" the white South from corruption, misgovernment, and northern and black control
         a. Violence was in broad daylight
    G. The Disputed Election and Bargain of 1877
       1. The Election between Rutherford B. Hayes and Samuel Tilden was very close
       2. Congress intervened
       3. Hayes won the election through a compromise
       4. Reconstruction ended in 1877
       5. Even while it lasted, however, Reconstruction revealed some of the tensions inherent in the nineteenth-century discussions of freedom

## SUGGESTED DISCUSSION QUESTIONS

- There were many proposals for various land reforms. Describe the various plans, why they did not work, and the consequences of their failure. Discuss the petition to Andrew Johnson in *Voices of Freedom*.
- Describe Lincoln's plan for Reconstruction. How was his plan a reflection of his adherence to preserving the Union?
- What course did presidential Reconstruction take? How did the South respond?
- What did freedom mean to the blacks? How did they express their newfound freedom?
- What made the Radical Republicans "radical"?
- Discuss Charles Sumner's remark that rather than a threat to liberty, the federal government had become "the custodian of freedom."
- Why did Reconstruction come to end in 1877?

## SUPPLEMENTAL WEB AND VISUAL RESOURCES

Andrew Johnson
*www.grolier.com/presidents/ea/bios/17pjhnsn.html*
This site focuses on the American presidency in general but has a helpful biography on Andrew Johnson. Included are recommended readings and links to other material.

Fourteenth Amendment
*www.grolier.com/presidents/ea/bios/17pjhnsn.html*
The Fourteenth Amendment is well documented on this site with annotations at the bottom of the page.

Reconstruction Act
*www.ncrepublic.org/recon3.html*

This North Carolina American Republic Web site contains plenty of links to other relevant material concerning the Reconstruction Act.

Ku Klux Klan
*www.spartacus.schoolnet.co.uk/USAkkk.htm*
This is an excellent site that covers the history of the Ku Klux Klan.

Black Communities after the Civil War
*www.films.com/Films_Home/item.cfm?s=1&bin=8346*
This film concentrates on black communities after the Civil War and includes the increasing violence that occurred from the Ku Klux Klan.

## SUPPLEMENTAL PRINT RESOURCES

Bond, James. *No Easy Walk to Freedom: Reconstruction and the Ratification of the Fourteenth Amendment.* Westport, CT: Praeger, 1997.

Brown, Elsa Barkley. "Negotiating and Transforming the Public Sphere: African American Political Life in the Transition from Slavery to Freedom." *Public Culture* 7 (1994): 107–146.

Cimbala, Paul. *Under the Guardianship of the Nation: The Freedmen's Bureau and the Reconstruction of Georgia, 1865–1870.* Athens: University of Georgia Press, 1997.

Duncan, Russell. *Freedom's Shore: Tunis Campbell and the Georgia Freedmen.* Athens: University of Georgia Press, 1987.

Foner, Eric. *Nothing But Freedom: Emancipation and Its Legacy.* Baton Rouge: Louisiana State University Press, 1983.

McPherson, James. *Abraham Lincoln and the Second American Revolution.* New York: Oxford University Press, 1991.

## TEST BANK

### Matching

| | | |
|---|---|---|
| f | 1. Thaddeus Stevens | a. secretary of war |
| c | 2. Andrew Johnson | b. proposed the Civil Rights Bill of 1866 |
| j | 3. Charles Sumner | c. presidential Reconstruction |
| h | 4. Rutherford B. Hayes | d. Liberal Republicans' presidential candidate |
| a | 5. Edwin Stanton | e. first black Senator |
| i | 6. Elizabeth Cady Stanton | f. Radical Republican congressman from Pennsylvania |
| b | 7. Lyman Trumbull | g. Whiskey Ring |

| | | |
|---|---|---|
| e | 8. Hiram Revels | h. ended Reconstruction |
| g | 9. Ulysses S. Grant | i. National Woman Suffrage Association |
| d | 10. Horace Greeley | j. Radical Republican senator from Massachusetts |

| | | |
|---|---|---|
| c | 1. Special Field Order 15 | a. restrictions placed on freed blacks in South |
| d | 2. carpetbaggers | b. home rule |
| g | 3. Howard University | c. "40 acres and a mule" |
| i | 4. scalawags | d. northerners who came to the South during Reconstruction |
| a | 5. Black Codes | e. ended Reconstruction |
| j | 6. Ten-Percent Plan | f. government agency that helped blacks in South |
| b | 7. redeemers | g. black school in Washington, D.C. |
| e | 8. Compromise of 1877 | h. terror organization |
| f | 9. Freedmen's Bureau | i. white southern Republican |
| h | 10. Ku Klux Klan | j. Lincoln's plan for Reconstruction |

## Multiple Choice

1. The Special Field Order 15 issued by General Sherman
   a. gave freed slaves the right to find their family members who had been sold away
   *b. set aside the Sea Islands and forty-acre tracts of land in South Carolina and Georgia for black families
   c. gave "40 acres and a mule" to blacks who wished to move to the unsettled American Southwest
   d. gave his army instructions to burn their way through the South to the coast
   e. established the Freedmen's Bureau to help blacks make the transition from slavery to freedom

2. Which of the following *best* describes the black response to the ending of the Civil War and the coming of freedom?
   a. Sensing the continued hatred of whites toward them, most blacks wished to move back to Africa
   b. Most blacks stayed with their old masters because they were not familiar with any other opportunities
   *c. Blacks adopted different ways of testing their freedom, including moving about, seeking kin, and rejecting older forms of deferential behavior
   d. Desiring better wages, most blacks moved to the northern cities to seek factory work

    e. Most blacks were content working for wages and not owning their own land because they believed that they had not earned the right to just be given land from the government

3. With slavery dead, which black institution strengthened after the war?
    a. the free blacks' church
    b. the secret slave church
    c. the black family
    d. the free blacks' schools
   *e. all of the above

4. The Freedmen's Bureau's greatest achievements were in
   *a. education and health care
    b. legal representation and employment
    c. land redistribution and law enforcement
    d. prosecuting Confederates and rebuilding southern infrastructure
    e. suffrage for blacks and citizenship for blacks

5. Lincoln's plan for Reconstruction was based upon
   *a. ten percent of the 1860 electorate taking an oath of allegiance to the Union
    b. confiscating southern land and redistributing it to the ex-slaves under the slogan "40 acres and a mule."
    c. a military occupation of the South until the southern states wrote new constitutions guaranteeing black suffrage
    d. ratifying the Fourteenth Amendment
    e. presidential pardons for the former Confederate leadership so that they might regain office in Congress

6. Which statement about Andrew Johnson is false?
    a. Johnson identified himself as the champion of the "honest yeomen" and a foe of large planters
   *b. Johnson campaigned for the ratification of the Fourteenth Amendment, against his Party's wishes
    c. Johnson lacked Lincoln's political skills and keen sense of public opinion
    d. Johnson believed that African-Americans had no role to play in Reconstruction
    e. Johnson's plan for Reconstruction offered pardons to the white southern elite

7. The "Black Codes" of the South
    a. declared black suffrage
    b. were a series of steps outlined by the Freedmen's Bureau to gain employment
    c. were codes of conduct that ex-slaves developed to demonstrate their Christianity and education

    \*d. resembled old slave codes and placed many restrictions upon ex-slaves' freedom

    e. were denounced by President Johnson and ruled to be unconstitutional by the Supreme Court

8. The most ambitious, but least successful of the Radical Republicans' aims was
   - \*a. land reform
   - b. black suffrage
   - c. federal protection of civil rights
   - d. public education
   - e. reunification of the Union

9. Andrew Johnson vetoed the 1866 Civil Rights Act because
   - a. he believed that the protection of civil rights was a federal responsibility, not one for the states
   - b. it did not include suffrage for blacks, something he thought was needed
   - \*c. he did not believe that blacks deserved the rights of citizenship
   - d. he was angry at Congress and refused to pass any of its legislation
   - e. none of the above

10. The Fourteenth Amendment
    - a. abolished slavery
    - b. guaranteed that suffrage could not be denied on account of race
    - c. severely punished the ex-Confederates
    - d. established the Freedmen's Bureau
    - \*e. declared that anyone born or naturalized in the United States was a citizen

11. The Naturalization act of 1790 and the *Dred Scott* decision both illustrate that prior to the Civil War, citizenship had been closely linked to
    - \*a. race
    - b. property ownership
    - c. gender
    - d. freedom
    - e. birthplace

12. The passage of the Fifteenth Amendment
    - a. split the feminist movement into two major organizations
    - b. had been bitterly opposed by the Democratic Party
    - c. marked the end of the American Antislavery Society, as its work was now complete
    - d. left many loopholes for the South to disfranchise blacks
    - \*e. all of the above

13. Elizabeth Cady Stanton and Susan B. Anthony founded the
    - \*a. National Woman Suffrage Association

    b. Women's Christian Temperance Union

    c. first Settlement House

    d. Equal Rights Association

    e. Fifteenth Amendment Advocacy Society

14. Hiram Revels and Blanche Bruce were the first two black
    a. congressmen
    b. governors
    c. mayors
  *d. senators
    e. federal judges

15. Carpetbaggers and scalawags
    a. were out for personal gain, taking advantage of Reconstruction
    b. were Democrats who wanted to help the blacks in the South
    c. were largely ignored and unsuccessful in the South
  *d. were northern and southern Republicans who sought political office in the South
    e. were terror groups who advocated violence toward blacks in the South

16. What was not an accomplishment of the Republicans in the South during Reconstruction?
    a. state-supported public schools
  *b. land reform
    c. pioneering civil rights legislation
    d. finance of railroad construction in the region
    e. tax incentives to attract northern manufacturers to invest in the region

17. Liberal Republicans believed that
  *a. power in the South should be returned to the region's "natural leaders"
    b. it was the responsibility of the federal government to continue assisting blacks
    c. President Grant was a brilliant politician
    d. Thaddeus Stevens would be their best presidential hope in 1876
    e. Congress had to stay committed to the Reconstruction cause

18. Who claimed to have converted the white South from corruption, misgovernment, and northern and black control?
    a. Republicans
    b. carpetbaggers
  *c. redeemers
    d. scalawags
    e. Ku Klux Klan

19. The election of 1876
    a. was won by Rutherford B. Hayes by a landslide
    b. was finally decided by the Supreme Court

    c. marked the final stage of Reconstruction, which ended in 1880
*d. was close and tainted by claims of fraud in Florida, South Carolina, and Louisiana
    e. was won by Ulysses S. Grant by a narrow count

20. The Bargain of 1877
    a. allowed Samuel Tilden to become president
*b. ended Reconstruction
    c. marked a compromise between Radical and Liberal Republicans
    d. called for the passage of the Fifteenth Amendment
    e. was made by Grant to end the Whiskey Ring

## True or False

T    1. Black ministers during Reconstruction played a major role in politics, holding some 250 public offices.

T    2. The Civil War was devastating to the South, which lost nearly one-fifth of its adult white male population.

F    3. Because of land redistribution, the vast majority of rural freed people prospered during Reconstruction.

F    4. By the mid-1870s, white farmers were cultivating as much as 80 percent of the South's cotton crop.

T    5. By and large, white voters in the South returned prominent Confederates and members of the old elite to power during presidential Reconstruction.

F    6. Compared to the rest of world history, the rebels of the defeated Confederacy were treated very harshly.

T    7. Thaddeus Stevens's most cherished aim was to confiscate the land of disloyal planters and divide it among former slaves and northern migrants to the South.

T    8. The Civil Rights Act of 1866 became the first major law in American history to be passed over a presidential veto.

F    9. The Senate, following the House's impeachment, removed Andrew Johnson from office.

F    10. With the passage of the Fourteenth Amendment, all peoples born in the United States were automatically citizens, including the Chinese, who had previously been barred from citizenship.

T    11. Lucy Stone favored the Fifteenth Amendment and established the American Woman Suffrage Association.

F  12. When the Union was restored by 1870, the southern states held Democratic majorities.

F  13. Black suffrage made little difference in the South as very few blacks ran for public office.

F  14. Since Reconstruction, both the House of Representatives and the Senate have had at least one black member.

T  15. White southern Democrats considered scalawags traitors to both their party and race.

T  16. While Republicans were in power in the South, they established the region's first state-supported public schools.

T  17. Opponents of Radical Reconstruction could not accept the idea of former slaves voting, holding office, and enjoying equality before the law.

F  18. The Ku Klux Klan was an organization of the lower classes of the South—those who felt left out of white society.

T  19. In Mississippi, in 1875, white rifle clubs drilled in public and openly assaulted and murdered Republicans.

F  20. The 1873 depression strengthened the North's resolve to ensure the success of Reconstruction since the depression really hurt the South's farmers, highlighting the need for reform in the region.

## Short Answer

*Identify and give the historical significance of each of the following terms, events, and people in a paragraph or two.*

1. Fourteenth Amendment
2. Ku Klux Klan
3. Wade-Davis Bill
4. Andrew Johnson
5. sharecropping

6. Radical Republicans
7. Black Codes
8. Freedmen's Bureau
9. Fifteenth Amendment
10. redeemers

## Essay Questions

1. What did "freedom" mean for the ex-slaves? Be sure to address economic opportunities, gender roles, religious independence, and family security.

2. Why did Radical Republicans believe that Andrew Johnson would support their agenda? Why was Johnson ultimately unable to lend his support to the Civil Rights Act of 1866 or the Fourteenth Amendment?

3. For whites, freedom, no matter how defined, was a given, a birthright to be defended. For African-Americans, it was an open-ended process, a transformation of every aspect of their lives and of the society and culture that had sustained slavery in the first place. Defend this statement.

4. Explain how wartime devastation set in motion a chain of events that permanently altered the white yeomanry's independent way of life, leading to what they considered a loss of freedom.

5. Reconstruction witnessed profound changes in the lives of southerners, black and white, rich and poor. Explain the various ways that the lives of these groups were changed. How were the changes for the better or worse?

6. Stating that he "lived among men, not among angels," Thaddeus Stevens recognized that the Fourteenth Amendment was not perfect. Explain the strengths and weaknesses of the Fourteenth Amendment. What liberties and freedoms does it extend? Describe how it gave more power to the federal government at the expense of the states.

7. What faults did the Republicans see with presidential Reconstruction? How did they propose to rectify those deficiencies? Be sure to distinguish moderate Republicans from Radical Republicans in your answer.

8. Who were the redeemers, what did they want, and what were their methods? How did the redeemers feel that their freedom was being threatened? Conclude your essay with a comment on how you think the federal government should have responded to the redeemers.

9. Analyze whether or not "40 acres and a mule" would have made a difference in the outcome of Reconstruction.

10. Fully discuss the successes and failures of Reconstruction. Be sure to explain how freedom was expanded or constricted for various groups of people.

America's Gilded Age, 1870–1890

This chapter concentrates on the history of America's industrial revolution and the settlement of the West in the late nineteenth century. The chapter opens with the dedication of the Statue of Liberty, a national symbol of the freedom for which America stands. However, the Gilded Age revealed that the nation had not yet decided what role the government should play in guaranteeing those freedoms. The industrial revolution brought tremendous urban growth, created a national market, and made captains of industry very rich while exploiting the working class. Farming was transformed too, and the settlement of the West after the Civil War resulted in the displacement of American Indians. Fighting to keep their land and freedom, the Indians fought the American cavalry in a series of wars culminating at Wounded Knee. Chief Joseph unsuccessfully led his people toward Canada, hoping to escape being placed on a reservation. His story is told in *Voices of Freedom*. Next, the chapter discusses the politics of Gilded Age, a period of political stalemate, inaction, and corrupt city machines. Freedom in the Gilded Age is explored, looking closely at Social Darwinism, the concept of "liberty of contract," and the courts' participation in defining freedom during the industrial age. Responding to the hardships of industrialization were the Knights of Labor and various social critics such as Henry George, Edward Bellamy, and Walter Rauschenbusch. The chapter concludes with the Haymarket Affair and Henry George's run for New York City mayor, indicating that labor was attempting to become a permanent political force by the end of the Gilded Age.

## CHAPTER OUTLINE

I. The Statue of Liberty

II. The Second Industrial Revolution
   A. The Industrial Economy

    1. By 1913, the United States produced one-third of the world's industrial output

    2. The 1880 census showed for the first time that a majority of the work force engaged in non-farming jobs

    3. Growth of cities were vital for financing industrialization

       a. Great Lakes region

          i. Pittsburgh

          ii. Chicago

B. The National Market

    1. The railroad made possible what is sometimes called the second industrial revolution

    2. The growing population formed an ever-expanding market for the mass production, mass distribution, and mass marketing of goods

C. The Spirit of Innovation

    1. Scientific breakthroughs poured forth from Thomas A. Edison

D. Competition and Consolidation

    1. Depression plagued the economy between 1873 and 1897

    2. Businesses engaged in ruthless competition

    3. To avoid cutthroat competition, more and more corporations battled to control entire industries

       a. Between 1897 and 1904, 4,000 firms vanished into larger corporations

E. Captains of Industry

    1. The railroad pioneered modern techniques of business organization

       a. Thomas Scott of Pennsylvania Railroad

    2. Andrew Carnegie worked for Scott at Pennsylvania Railroad

    3. By the 1890s, Carnegie dominated the steel industry

       a. Vertical integration

    4. Carnegie's life reflected his desire to succeed and his desire to give back to society

    5. John D. Rockefeller dominated the oil industry

       a. Horizontal integration

    6. "Captains of industry" versus "Robber Barons"

F. Workers' Freedom in an Industrial Age

    1. For a minority of workers, the rapidly expanding industrial system created new forms of freedom

    2. For most workers, economic insecurity remained a basic fact of life

    3. Between 1880 and 1900, an average of 35,000 workers perished each year in factory and mine accidents, the highest rate in the industrial world

    4. Women were part of the working class

G. Sunshine and Shadow

    1. Class divisions became more and more visible

      2. Many of the wealthiest Americans consciously pursued an aristocratic lifestyle

         a. Thorstein Veblen on "conspicuous consumption"

      3. The working class lived in desperate conditions

III. The Transformation of the West

    A. A Farming Empire

      1. More land came into cultivation in the thirty years after the Civil War than in the previous two-and-a-half centuries of American history

      2. Even small farmers became increasingly oriented to national and international markets

      3. As crop production increased, prices fell and small farmers throughout the world suffered severe difficulties in the last quarter of the nineteenth century

      4. The future of western farming ultimately lay with giant agricultural enterprises

    B. The Day of the Cowboy

      1. The cowboys became symbols of a life of freedom on the open range

    C. The Corporate West

      1. Many western industries fell under the sway of companies that mobilized eastern and European investment to introduce advanced technology

      2. New Mexican sheepfarming

    D. The Subjugation of the Plains Indians

      1. The incorporation of the West into the national economy spelled the doom of the Plains Indians and their world

      2. As settlers encroached on Indian lands, bloody conflict between the army and Plains tribes began in the 1850s and continued until 1890

      3. The Union army launched a campaign against the Navajo in the Southwest

      4. Once numbering 30 million in 1800, buffalo were nearly extinct from hunting by 1890

    E. Let Me Be a Free Man

      1. The Nez Perce were chased over 1,700 miles before surrendering in 1877

      2. Chief Joseph spoke of freedom before a distinguished audience in 1879

      3. Defending their land, Sioux and Cheyenne warriors attacked Custer at Little Big Horn

      4. These events delayed only temporarily the onward march of white soldiers, settlers, and prospectors

    F. Remaking Indian Life

      1. In 1871, Congress eliminated the treaty system that dated back to the Revolutionary era

         a. Forced assimilation

2. The crucial step in attacking "tribalism" came in 1887 with the passage of the Dawes Act
   a. The policy proved to be a disaster for the Indians
G. The Ghost Dance and Wounded Knee
   1. Some Indians sought solace in the Ghost Dance, a religious revitalization campaign reminiscent of the pan-Indian movements led by earlier prophets like Neolin and Tenskwatawa
   2. On December 29, 1890, soldiers opened fire on Ghost Dancers encamped on Wounded Knee Creek in South Dakota, killing between 150 and 200 Indians, mostly women and children

IV. Politics in a Gilded Age
  A. The Corruption of Politics
     1. Americans during the Gilded Age saw their nation as an island of political democracy in a world still dominated by undemocratic governments
     2. Political corruption was rife
     3. Urban politics fell under the sway of corrupt political machines
        a. Boss Tweed
     4. Corruption was at the national level too
        a. Credit Mobilier
  B. The Politics of Dead Center
     1. Every Republican candidate for president from 1868 to 1900 had fought in the Union army
        a. Union soldiers' pensions
     2. Democrats dominated the South and Catholic votes
     3. The parties were closely divided and national elections were very close
     4. Gilded Age presidents made little effort to mobilize public opinion or exert executive leadership
     5. In some ways, American democracy in the Gilded Age seemed remarkably healthy
  C. Government and the Economy
     1. The nation's political structure proved ill-equipped to deal with the problems created by the economy's rapid growth
        a. Tariff policy was debated
        b. Return to gold standard in 1879
     2. Republican economic policies strongly favored the interests of eastern industrialists and bankers
     3. The Civil Service Act of 1883 created a merit system for federal employees
     4. Congress established the Interstate Commerce Commission (ICC) in 1887
        a. Sherman Antitrust Act

    D. Political Conflict in the States
1. State governments expanded their responsibilities to the public
2. Third parties enjoyed significant, if short-lived, success in local elections
    a. The Greenback-Labor Party
3. Farmers responded to railroad policies by organizing the Grange
4. Some states passed eight-hour-day laws

V. Freedom in the Gilded Age
  A. The Social Problem
1. As the United States matured into an industrial economy, Americans struggled to make sense of the new social order
2. Many Americans sensed that something had gone wrong in the nation's social development
  B. Freedom, Inequality, and Democracy
1. Many Americans viewed the concentration of wealth as inevitable, natural, and justified by progress
2. Gilded Age reformers feared that with lower-class groups seeking to use government to advance their own interests, democracy was becoming a threat to individual liberty and the rights of property
  C. Social Darwinism in America
1. Charles Darwin put forth the theory of evolution whereby plant and animal species best suited to their environment took the place of those less able to adapt
2. Social Darwinism argued that evolution was as natural a process in human society as in nature, and government must not interfere
3. Failure to advance in society was widely thought to indicate a lack of character
4. Social Darwinist William Sumner believed that freedom required frank acceptance of inequality
  D. Liberty of Contract
1. Labor contracts reconciled freedom and authority in the workplace
2. Demands by workers that the government help them struck liberals as an example of how the misuse of political power posed a threat to liberty
  E. The Courts and Freedom
1. The courts viewed state regulation of business as an insult to free labor
2. The courts generally sided with business enterprises that complained of a loss of economic freedom
3. *Lochner v. New York* voided a state law establishing ten hours per day or sixty per week as the maximum hours of work for bakers, citing that it infringed upon individual freedom

VI. Labor and the Republic
    A. The Overwhelming Labor Question
        1. The 1877 Great Railroad Strike demonstrated that there was an "overwhelming labor question"
    B. The Knights of Labor in an Industrial Age
        1. The Knights of Labor organized all workers to improve social conditions
    C. The Conditions Essential to Liberty
        1. Labor raised the question whether meaningful freedom could exist in a situation of extreme economic inequality
    D. Middle-Class Reformers
        1. Alarmed by fear of class warfare and the growing power of concentrated capital, social thinkers offered numerous plans for change
    E. Progress and Poverty
        1. Henry George's solution was the "single tax"
        2. George rejected the traditional equation of liberty with ownership of land
    F. Gronlund and Bellamy
        1. Lawrence Gronlund's *Cooperative Commonwealth* was the first book to popularize socialist ideas for an American audience
        2. It explained socialist concepts in easy-to-understand prose
        3. Freedom, Edward Bellamy insisted, was a social condition, resting on interdependence, not autonomy
        4. Bellamy held out the hope of retaining the material abundance made possible by industrial capitalism while eliminating inequality
    G. A Social Gospel
        1. Walter Rauschenbusch insisted that freedom and spiritual self-development required an equalization of wealth and power and that unbridled competition mocked the Christian ideal of brotherhood
        2. Social Gospel adherents established mission and relief programs in urban areas
    H. The Haymarket Affair
        1. On May 1, 1886, some 350,000 workers in cities across the country demonstrated for an eight-hour day
        2. A riot ensued after a bomb killed a police officer on May 4
        3. Employers took the opportunity to paint the labor movement as a dangerous and un-American force prone to violence and controlled by foreign-born radicals
        4. Seven of the eight men accused of plotting the Haymarket bombing were foreign-born
    I. Labor and Politics
        1. Henry George ran for mayor of New York in 1886 on a labor ticket
        2. The events of 1886 suggested that labor might be on the verge of establishing itself as a permanent political force

## SUGGESTED DISCUSSION QUESTIONS

- Students often believe that the United States suffered through a Great Depression only in the 1930s. Ask them to discuss the effects of the first Great Depression between 1873 and 1897. What caused it? How did Labor respond?
- How does the emergence of the Ghost Dance reflect the experiences of the Indians? What was the significance of Wounded Knee?
- Read Chief Joseph's speech in *Voices of Freedom*, and explain his argument. How did he employ the concept of freedom?
- Explain the reasoning behind the Supreme Court's rulings in regard to industry. How was the Court defining freedom?
- Who were America's new industrial workers?
- What factors contributed to the rise of the labor movement in the nineteenth century?

## SUPPLEMENTAL WEB AND VISUAL SOURCES

The Way West
*www.current.org/hi/hi411.html*
Part of the PBS series "The American Experience," *The Way West* tells the story of how the West was lost and won from the time of the Gold Rush until after the last gasp of the Indian Wars at Wounded Knee. Four Volumes. Written and directed by Ric Burns.

Thomas Edison
*www.thomasedison.com/*
This site has a complete biography of Thomas Edison, a detailed list of inventions and a photo gallery.

Andrew Carnegie
*www.pbs.org/wgbh/amex/carnegie/*
From the PBS series "The American Experience," this film is titled *The Richest Man in the World: Andrew Carnegie*.

John D. Rockefeller
*voteview.uh.edu/entrejdr.htm*
This site covers every major event from Rockefeller's rags-to-riches life. It includes various graphs of earnings of the Standard Oil Company.

Chief Joseph
*www.pbs.org/weta/thewest/people/a_c/chiefjoseph.htm*
*The West*, an eight-part documentary series from PBS, has valuable resources at this site. It includes a biography of Chief Joseph and cites a variety of his speeches.

Wounded Knee
*www.ibiscom.com/knee.htm*
This site documents the massacre of Wounded Knee and includes pictures and references.

## SUPPLEMENTAL PRINT RESOURCES

Brown, Dee. *Bury My Heart At Wounded Knee.* New York: Henry Holt, 1970.

Campbell, Ballard, ed. *The Human Tradition in The Gilded Age and Progressive Era.* Wilmington, DE: Scholarly Resources, 2000.

Huhndorf, Shari. *Going Native: Indians in the American Cultural Imagination.* Ithaca: Cornell University Press, 2001.

Igler, David. *Industrial Cowboys: Miller & Lux and the Transformation of the Far West, 1850–1920.* Berkeley: University of California Press, 2001.

Kazin, Michael, and Steven Ross. "America's Labor Day: The Dilemma of a Workers' Celebration." *Journal of American History* 78, no. 4 (1992): 1294–1323.

Kens, Paul. *Lochner v. New York: Economic Regulation on Trial.* Lawrence: University of Kansas Press, 1998.

Numbers, Ronald. *Darwinism Comes to America.* Cambridge: Harvard University Press, 1998.

Summers, Mark Wahlgren. *The Gilded Age: Or, The Hazard of New Functions.* New York: Prentice Hall, 1997.

Wilson, R. Jackson. "Experience and Utopia: The Making of Edward Bellamy's *Looking Backward*." *Journal of American Studies* 11, no. 1 (1977): 45–60.

## TEST BANK

### Matching

| | | | |
|---|---|---|---|
| f | 1. Thomas Edison | a. | Social Gospel movement |
| e | 2. Thomas Scott | b. | steel industrial giant |
| b | 3. Andrew Carnegie | c. | Nez Perce |
| j | 4. John D. Rockefeller | d. | Knights of Labor |
| i | 5. William G. Sumner | e. | Pennsylvania Railroad |
| d | 6. Terence Powderly | f. | inventor |
| h | 7. Edward Bellamy | g. | Buffalo Bill's Wild West show |
| a | 8. Walter Rauschenbusch | h. | utopian novelist |
| c | 9. Chief Joseph | i. | Social Darwinist |
| g | 10. Sitting Bull | j. | oil industry giant |

| | | |
|---|---|---|
| d | 1. trusts | a. merit system for federal employees |
| g | 2. vertical integration | b. believed that equality of wealth was required for freedom |
| f | 3. horizontal integration | c. a corrupt political machine |
| b | 4. Social Gospel | d. a combination of corporations to establish a monopoly |
| h | 5. Dawes Act | e. covered in gold |
| i | 6. conspicuous consumption | f. buying out one's competitors |
| a | 7. Civil Service Act | g. controlling every phase of a business |
| e | 8. gilded | h. broke up tribal lands |
| j | 9. Social Darwinism | i. spending money simply to show off wealth |
| c | 10. Tweed Ring | j. survival of the fittest |

## Multiple Choice

1. What was not a cause for the explosive economic growth experienced by the United States between 1870 and 1890?
    a. availability of capital for investment
    b. a growing supply of labor
    c. abundant natural resources
    *d. low tariffs
    d. federal land grants to railroads

2. Which city became the world's center for iron and steel manufacturing?
    a. Chicago
    b. New York
    c. Buffalo
    d. Cleveland
    *e. Pittsburgh

3. The _____ made possible the second industrial revolution in America.
    a. oil industry
    *b. railroads
    c. iron industry
    d. textiles
    e. cotton gin

4. The American working class
    a. were paid less than their European counterparts
    b. worked in safe conditions and fatal factory accidents were uncommon
    c. did not include women and children
    d. was quickly making gains and moving into the middle class
    *e. lived in desperate conditions

5. An example of what economist and social historian Thorstein Veblen meant by "conspicuous consumption" is
   *a. Mrs. Bradley Martin's costume ball
   b. an immigrant's purchase of bread
   c. the free services handed out by social reformers
   d. John Rockefeller's purchase of one of his competitors' companies
   e. the social welfare services of European nations like Germany

6. The Dawes Act
   a. placed Indians on reservations
   *b. divided tribal lands into parcels of land for Indian families
   c. outlawed the killing of buffalo
   d. was considered a success by the Indians
   e. ended the Indian Wars in the West

7. What event marked the end of the Indian Wars?
   a. Battle of Little Big Horn
   b. surrender of Chief Joseph and the Nez Perce
   *c. Battle of Wounded Knee
   d. establishment of the Ghost Dance
   e. surrender of Sitting Bull

8. William Tweed was
   *a. a political "boss" who, although corrupt, provided important services to New Yorkers
   b. a civic reformer who introduced a clean, non-partisan form of government in New York
   c. an infamous precinct worker in Chicago who made millions off the immigrants
   d. a corrupt landlord of tenement-style urban residences in Pittsburgh
   e. a socialist who ran for Mayor of New York on the Labor Party ticket

9. Republican economic policies strongly favored
   a. midwestern farmers
   b. southern sharecroppers
   c. national consumers
   *d. eastern industrialists and bankers
   e. western silver mine owners

13. Social Darwinism in America
   a. evolved from the British philosopher Herbert Spencer
   b. argued that evolution was as natural a process in human society as in nature, and government must not interfere
   c. argued that failure to advance in society indicated a lack of character
   d. argued that freedom required frank acceptance of inequality
   *e. all of the above

14. What did William Graham Sumner believe social classes owed each other?
    a. cooperation to move ahead
    b. a redistribution of wealth
    *c. nothing at all
    d. respect and equality
    e. a spirit of kinship to fix the ills of society together

15. Which statement about labor and the law is false?
    a. The courts viewed state regulation of business as an insult to free labor
    b. *Lochner v. New York* voided a state law that established maximum working hours for bakers, citing that it infringed upon individual freedom
    c. The courts generally sided with business enterprises that complained of a loss of economic freedom
    *d. Workers generally welcomed the courts' decisions on industry
    e. Liberals thought that the workers' demands that the government help them was an example of how the misuse of political power posed a threat to liberty

16. One of the reasons that the Great Strike of 1877 was important is that
    a. not since the Civil War had so many people been killed
    *b. it underscored the tensions produced by the rapid industrialization of the time
    c. the victory won by labor was the greatest for the labor movement in American history
    d. it proved the theory of Social Darwinism
    e. it demonstrated how effective the Knights of Labor could be in organizing workers

17. Henry George rejected the traditional equation of liberty with
    *a. ownership of land
    b. the right to vote
    c. equal access to wealth
    d. race
    e. the right to work

18. Who insisted that freedom and spiritual self-development required an equalization of wealth and power and that unbridled competition mocked the Christian ideal of brotherhood?
    a. Andrew Carnegie
    *b. Walter Rauschenbusch
    c. Herbert Spencer
    d. William Graham Sumner
    e. William Tweed

19. Which statement about the Haymarket Affair is false?
    a. A bomb exploded, killing a police officer

&ast;b. The Knights of Labor were directly responsible for the violence that took place at Haymarket

c. Employers took the opportunity to paint the labor movement as a dangerous and un-American force prone to violence and controlled by foreign-born radicals

d. Seven of the eight men accused of plotting the Haymarket bombing were foreign-born

e. Laborers were gathered at Haymarket Square to demonstrate for an eight-hour day

20. Who ran for mayor of New York in 1886 on a labor ticket?
    a. Edward Bellamy
    b. Horace Greeley
    &ast;c. Henry George
    d. George Plunkitt
    e. Walter Rauschenbusch

## True or False

T    1. The idea for the Statue of Liberty originated as a response to the assassination of Abraham Lincoln.

F    2. By the turn of the century, most Americans still worked for themselves as small business owners or farmers.

F    3. In order to reduce accidents along the railways, the federal government officially divided the nation into four time zones in 1883.

F    4. The economy surged forward between 1870 and 1890, bringing prosperity and growth with only minor hiccups.

T    5. The spread of electricity was essential to industrial and urban growth.

T    6. Both Andrew Carnegie and John D. Rockefeller amassed huge fortunes through vertical integration.

T    7. American workers received higher pay than their European counterparts, but their working conditions were more dangerous.

F    8. The Dawes Act was an extension of the treaty system practiced by the American government since the Revolutionary War.

F    9. The Battle of Little Big Horn resulted in the massacre of over 100 Indians.

T    10. Boss Tweed led a corrupt political machine in New York.

T    11. Grover Cleveland was a Democrat who served nonconsecutive terms and whose small staff allowed him the occasional opportunity to answer the White House door.

F    12. Since national elections were always so close, voter participation in the Gilded Age was never over 60 percent.

T    13. Republican economic policies strongly favored the interests of eastern industrialists and bankers.

T    14. Gilded Age reformers feared that with lower-class groups seeking to use government to advance their own interests, democracy was becoming a threat to individual liberty and the rights of property.

F    15. William Graham Sumner believed that the role of government extended to helping the poor.

T    16. Demands by workers that the government help them struck liberals as an example of how the misuse of political power posed a threat to liberty.

T    17. *Lochner v. New York* voided a state law establishing ten hours per day or sixty per week as the maximum hours of work for bakers, citing that it infringed upon individual freedom.

T    18. Labor raised the question of whether meaningful freedom could exist in a situation of extreme economic inequality.

F    19. *Looking Backward* was the first book to popularize socialist ideas for an American audience.

T    20. The events of 1886 suggested that labor might be on the verge of establishing itself as a permanent political force.

## Short Answer

*Identify and give the historical significance of each of the following terms, events, and people in a paragraph or two.*

1. vertical and horizontal integration
2. Henry George
3. Social Darwinism
4. Indian Wars
5. utopian and cataclysmic novels
6. Haymarket Square
7. Dawes Act
8. Social Gospel
9. "liberty of contract"
10. Knights of Labor

## Essay Questions

1. What are the social conditions that make freedom possible, and what role should the national government play in defining and protecting the liberty of its citizens?

2. Henry Demarest Lloyd wrote in *Wealth Against Commonwealth* (1864) that "Liberty and monopoly cannot live together." Is his statement true?

3. Describe how the industrial revolution created new forms of freedom for some workers while restricting some freedoms for others. What were the effects industrialization had upon workers? Be careful not to generalize all workers together.

4. What does the term "Gilded Age" mean? What did Mark Twain want to say about late-nineteenth-century America by using that term?

5. Sitting Bull stated, "The life my people want is a life of freedom." Describe what freedom meant to the Indians and how that conflicted with the interests and values of most white Americans.

6. As more and more economic inequality became apparent, the belief that freedom and equality were intricately linked seemed outdated. The task of social science was to devise a way to make men who were free, or equal in liberty, accept that there are inequalities in the distribution of wealth associated with industrialization. Explain the various ways reformers and social scientists devised to accomplish this task.

7. Union leader John Mitchell explained that the court system was guaranteeing liberties that the workers did not want and denying them the liberty that was of real value to them. Explain what he meant by this statement. How were the courts defining liberty and freedom?

8. How did the labor movement launch a sustained assault on the understanding of freedom grounded in Social Darwinism and the "liberty of contract"?

9. Write a dialogue between Terence Powderly and Andrew Carnegie on the impact of industrialization.

| CHAPTER 17 | Freedom's Boundaries, at Home and Abroad, 1890–1900 |

This chapter concentrates on the limitations of freedom, including that of farmers, immigrants, blacks, women, and colonial subjects. The chapter opens with the Homestead Strike, which demonstrated that neither a powerful union nor public opinion could influence the conduct of the largest corporations. Farmers also illustrated that not everyone benefited from the prosperity of the industrial revolution. The chapter examines how the farmers mobilized into a political force culminating in the 1892 organization of the Populist Party. Attempting to build a broad base, the Populists courted labor, women, and black farmers, but their party dissolved after the defeat of William Jennings Bryan in 1896. The chapter then explores the "New South." After Reconstruction blacks faced disenfranchisement, threat from the lynch rope, and Jim Crow laws sanctioned by the Supreme Court's decision on *Plessy v. Ferguson*. The "new" immigrants from southern and eastern Europe faced growing restrictions on their freedom in the face of nativism. The Chinese were singled out and permanently excluded from immigrating to America in 1882 and they had to fight through the court system to gain a few liberties. In *Voices of Freedom,* Chinese-American missionary Saum Song Bo highlights their plight in an ironic statement about freedom. Taking a different approach to the limitations of freedom put upon blacks was Booker T. Washington, who preached a policy of accommodation and vocational education. Likewise, the American Federation of Labor took a more realistic approach to unionization. Women, barred from suffrage, were nonetheless politically active in clubs and national organizations like the Women's Christian Temperance Union. All three groups, then, found ways to accommodate for the limitations placed upon them. The chapter ends by examining America's rise to world power. By expanding abroad in search of markets and new frontiers, America fought Spain in 1898 and won for itself a number of territorial possessions. With the annexation of the Philippines, Guam, and Puerto Rico, the United States took on an imperial role, restricting the freedoms of the Constitution to those peoples.

## CHAPTER OUTLINE

I. Homestead Strike

II. The Populist Challenge
   A. The Farmers' Revolt
      1. Farmers faced increasing economic insecurity
      2. Farmers sought to improve their condition through the Farmers Alliance
   B. The People's Party
      1. The People's, or Populist, Party emerged from the Farmers Alliance in the 1890s
         a. Spoke for all the "producing classes"
      2. The Populists embarked on a remarkable effort of community organization and education
      3. The Populist platform of 1892 remains a classic document of American reform
      4. Populists sought to rethink the relationship between freedom and government to address the crisis of the 1890s
   C. The Populist Coalition
      1. The Populists made remarkable efforts to unite black and white small farmers on a common political and economic program
         a. Colored Farmers Alliance
      2. While many blacks refused to abandon Lincoln's party others were attracted by the Populist appeal
      3. The Populist movement also engaged the energies of thousands of reform-minded women from farm and labor backgrounds
         a. Mary Elizabeth Lease
      4. 1892 president candidate James Weaver won over 1 million votes
   D. The Government and Labor
      1. The severe depression that began in 1893 led to increased conflict between capital and labor
         a. Coxey's Army
      2. Pullman strike of 1894 saw the labor leader Eugene Debs jailed
   E. Populism and Labor
      1. Populists made determined efforts to appeal to industrial workers but ultimately failed to get labor's support
      2. Instead of to the Populists, working-class voters in 1894 shifted en masse to the Republicans
   F. Bryan and Free Silver
      1. In 1896, Democrats and Populists joined to support William Jennings Bryan for the presidency
         a. Called for free silver
         b. Condemned the gold standard

G. The Campaign of 1896
  1. Republicans nominated Ohio governor William McKinley
  2. The election of 1896 is sometimes called the first modern presidential campaign
    a. Mark Hanna
  3. Some view L. Frank Baum's *The Wonderful Wizard of Oz* as a commentary on the election of 1896 and its aftermath
  4. McKinley's victory shattered the political stalemate that had persisted since 1876 and created one of the most enduring political majorities in American history

III. The Segregated South
  A. The Redeemers in Power
    1. On achieving power, Redeemers had moved to undo as much of Reconstruction as possible
      a. Public school systems hardest hit
    2. New laws authorized the arrest of virtually any person without employment and greatly increased the penalties for petty crimes
  B. The Failure of the New South Dream
    1. The region as a whole sank deeper and deeper into poverty
  C. Black Life in the South
    1. As the most disadvantaged rural southerners, black farmers suffered the most from the region's condition
      a. Blacks owned less land in 1900 than they had at the end of Reconstruction
    2. Cities supported the growth of a black middle class
    3. Most unions excluded blacks
  D. The Kansas Exodus
    1. African-Americans migrated to Kansas, seeking political equality, freedom from violence, access to education, and economic opportunity
    2. Most African-Americans had little alternative but to stay in the region
      a. Most northern employers refused to offer jobs to blacks
  E. The Decline of Black Politics
    1. Political opportunities became more and more restricted
    2. The banner of political leadership passed to black women activists
      a. The National Association of Colored Women
  F. The Elimination of Black Voting
    1. Some states saw coalitions between black Republicans and anti-Redeemer Democrats
    2. Between 1890 and 1906, every southern state enacted laws or constitutional provisions meant to eliminate the black vote
    3. Numerous poor and illiterate whites also lost the right to vote
    4. The elimination of black and many white voters could not have been accomplished without the approval of the North

G. The Law of Segregation
  1. In 1896, in the landmark *Plessy v. Ferguson* decision, the Supreme Court gave its approval to state laws requiring separate facilities for blacks and whites
  2. John Marshall Harlan was the lone dissenter on the Supreme Court
H. The Segregated South
  1. States reacted to the *Plessy* decision by passing laws mandating racial segregation in every aspect of southern life
    a. No black high school existed in the South by 1900
  2. The point was not so much to keep the races apart as to ensure that when they came into contact with each other whites held the upper hand
 I. The Rise of Lynching
  1. Those blacks who sought to challenge the system, or who refused to accept the demeaning behavior that was a daily feature of southern life, faced violence
  2. Many white southerners considered preserving the purity of white womanhood a justification of extralegal vengeance
    a. The charge of rape was a "bare lie"

IV. Redrawing the Boundaries
  A. The New Immigration and the New Nativism
    1. 3.5 million immigrants, mostly from southern and eastern Europe, arrived in the 1890s
      a. Viewed as inferior by native-born Americans
    2. Various suggestions were made by nativists to eliminate the immigrants' ability to vote
  B. Chinese Exclusion
    1. The Page Act barred Chinese women from entering the country
    2. Chinese Exclusion Act of 1882 barred Chinese from the United States
  C. The Rights of the Chinese
    1. Chinese demands for equal rights forced the Supreme Court to define the reach of the Fourteenth Amendment
      a. *Yick Wo v. Hopkins*
      b. *United States v. Wong Kim Ark*
    2. *Fong Yue Ting* (1893) authorized the federal government to expel Chinese aliens without due process of law
    3. Exclusion profoundly shaped the experience of Chinese-Americans
  D. The Emergence of Booker T. Washington
    1. Prominent black leaders took to emphasizing economic self-help and individual advancement into the middle class as an alternative to political agitation
    2. Washington emphasized vocational education over political equality
    3. He urged blacks not to try to combat segregation

E. The Rise of the American Federation of Labor (AFL)
   1. The rise of the AFL reflected a shift away from a broadly reformist past to more limited goals
   2. Samuel Gompers pioneered "business unionism"
   3. In the 1890s, the labor movement became less and less inclusive
F. The Woman's Era
   1. Changes in the women's movement reflected the same combination of expanding activities and narrowing boundaries
   2. Through a network of women's clubs, temperance associations, and social reform organizations, women exerted a growing influence on public affairs
      a. Women's Christian Temperance Union (WCTU)
   3. The center of gravity of feminism shifted toward an outlook more in keeping with prevailing racial and ethnic norms

V. Becoming a World Power
   A. American Expansionism
      1. America was a second-rate power in the 1880s
      2. Most Americans who looked overseas were interested in expanded trade, not territorial possessions
   B. The Lure of Empire
      1. A small group of late-nineteenth-century thinkers actively promoted American expansionism
         a. Josiah Strong
         b. Alfred T. Mahan
      2. Hawaii was long sought after by Americans
      3. The depression that began in 1893 heightened the belief that a more aggressive foreign policy was necessary to stimulate American exports
      4. Unifying patriotism dates to the 1890s
         a. The "cult of the flag"
         b. "Yellow press"
   C. The Splendid Little War
      1. Cuba had fought for independence since 1868
      2. The United States went to war with Spain to win Cuba's "liberty and freedom"
         a. Teller Amendment
      3. Admiral George Dewey defeated a Spanish fleet at Manila Bay
      4. Rough Riders took San Juan Hill in Cuba
         a. Teddy Roosevelt
   D. An American Empire
      1. In the treaty with Spain ending the war, the United States acquired the Philippines, Puerto Rico, and the Pacific island of Guam
         a. Platt Amendment for Cuba

      2. America's interest in its new possessions had more to do with trade than gaining wealth from natural resources or large-scale American settlement

      3. In 1899, Secretary of State John Hay announced the Open Door policy with China

E. The Philippine War

      1. Many believed that American participation in the destruction of Spanish rule would lead to social reform and political self-government

      2. Emilio Aguinaldo led a fight against American colonialism

      3. The McKinley administration justified its policies on the grounds that its aim was to "uplift and civilize and Christianize" the Filipinos

F. Citizens or Subjects?

      1. American rule also brought with it American racial attitudes

         a. "white man's burden"

      2. America's triumphant entry into the ranks of imperial powers sparked an intense debate over the relationship among political democracy, race, and American citizenship

      3. The Foraker Act of 1900 declared Puerto Rico an "insular territory," different from previous territories in the West

         a. The Insular Cases

      4. In the twentieth century, the territories acquired in 1898 would follow different paths

         a. Hawaii achieved statehood in 1959

         b. The Philippines got independence in 1946

         c. Puerto Rico is the "world's oldest colony" as a commonwealth

G. Republic or Empire?

      1. The Anti-Imperialist League argued that empire was incompatible with democracy

      2. But without any sense of contradiction, proponents of an imperial foreign policy also adopted the language of freedom

         a. Senator Albert Beveridge

      3. Brooks Adams's book *The New Empire* (1902) predicted that because of its economic power, the United States would soon "outweigh any single empire, if not all empires combined"

## SUGGESTED DISCUSSION QUESTIONS

- What caused workers to go on strike at Andrew Carnegie's Homestead Steel plant?
- Describe the plan of the Farmers' Alliance.
- What were the goals of the Populist Party? Why were they considered radical in their day?
- Who was Eugene Debs?

- Discuss Booker T. Washington's background and his plan for blacks. Does understanding his background help to explain the logic behind his message?
- What vehicle was still available to the Chinese to enlarge their freedoms after the passage of the Chinese Exclusion Act? Comment on the ironies apparent in the *Voices of Freedom* selection.
- What kind of empire did the United States create for itself? How would you describe it in comparison to other imperial powers of the day?

## SUPPLEMENTAL WEB AND VISUAL RESOURCES

Election of 1896
*www.turnmeondeadman.net/OZ/Populism.html*
This site attempts to link the 1896 election with *The Wonderful Wizard of Oz*.

William McKinley
*www.cohums.ohio-state.edu/history/projects/McKinley/*
This Ohio State Web site focuses on the era of President McKinley and includes political cartoons and pictures.

*Plessy v. Ferguson*
*campus.northpark.edu/history/WebChron/USA/PlessyFerguson.html*
This site from North Park University contains a segment on the *Plessy v. Ferguson* case with links to further research.

Booker T. Washington
*www.historycooperative.org/btw/*
This University of Illinois Press Web site contains volumes of information about Booker T. Washington, including searches and images.

Rough Riders
*www.bartleby.com/51/*
This site includes the book *Rough Riders,* taken from Teddy Roosevelt's personal writings on the Spanish American War.

Spanish American War
*www.films.com/Films_Home/item.cfm?s=1&bin=8335*
This site includes the video *The Spanish American War: A Conflict in Progress*.

## SUPPLEMENTAL PRINT RESOURCES

Daniels, Roger. *Not Like Us: Immigrants and Minorities in America, 1890–1924.* Chicago: Ivan R. Dee, 1997.
Dray, Philip. *At the Hands of Persons Unknown: The Lynching of Black America.* New York: Random House, 2002.

Leviatin, David, ed. *How The Other Half Lives.* New York: Bedford, 1996.

Takaki, Ronald. *Strangers From a Different Shore: A History of Asian Americans.* Boston: Back Bay Books, 1998.

Thomas, Brooke, ed. *Plessy v. Ferguson.* New York: Bedford, 1997.

Welke, Barbara Young. *Recasting American Liberty: Gender, Race, Law, and the Railroad Revolution.* New York: Cambridge University Press, 2001.

Wright, Gavin. "The Strange Career of the New Southern Economic History." *Reviews in American History* 10 (1982): 164–180.

## TEST BANK

### Matching

| | | |
|---|---|---|
| e | 1. Booker T. Washington | a. advocate of "free silver" |
| j | 2. Alfred T. Mahan | b. president of the American Railway Union |
| h | 3. Theodore Roosevelt | c. believed politics was the place for women |
| i | 4. Emilio Aguinaldo | d. Populist Party presidential candidate |
| a | 5. William Jennings Bryan | e. advocated vocational training for blacks |
| d | 6. James Weaver | f. Supreme Court justice |
| b | 7. Eugene Debs | g. pioneered "business unionism" |
| f | 8. John Marshall Harlan | h. fought with the Rough Riders |
| c | 9. Frances Willard | i. led the Filipino insurrection |
| g | 10. Samuel Gompers | j. promoted American expansionism via a navy |


| | | |
|---|---|---|
| h | 1. Homestead Strike | a. argued that the Constitution did not apply to territories |
| e | 2. Teller Amendment | b. excluded Chinese women from entering the United States |
| g | 3. disenfranchisement | c. "separate, but equal" |
| f | 4. Populist Party | d. warned that empire was incompatible with democracy |
| a | 5. Insular Cases | e. the United States was not to annex Cuba |
| j | 6. WCTU | f. politically active farmers |
| i | 7. Open Door policy | g. excluded from voting |
| d | 8. Liberty Tracts | h. labor unrest at a Carnegie steel mill |
| c | 9. *Plessy v. Ferguson* | i. effort to keep free trade in China |
| b | 10. Page Act | j. campaigned for temperance |

## Multiple Choice

1. Farmers believed that their plight derived from all of the following except
   a. high freight rates charged by railroads
   b. excessive interest rates for loans from bankers
   c. the high tariff policies of the federal government
   d. the fiscal policy that reduced the supply of money in the economy
   *e. the free and unlimited coinage of silver

2. Which statement about the People's Party is false?
   a. It emerged from the Farmers Alliance in the 1890s and claimed to speak for all the "producing classes"
   b. It embarked on a remarkable effort of community organization and education
   c. Its platform of 1892 remains a classic document of American reform, advocating radical ideas of the day such as graduated income tax and increased democracy
   *d. The Party emerged as an urban, middle-class vehicle for social, economic, and political reform
   e. It sought to rethink the relationship between freedom and government to address the crisis of the 1890s

3. Who was the 1892 presidential candidate for the Populist Party?
   a. Eugene Debs
   *b. James Weaver
   c. Jacob Coxey
   d. William Jennings Bryan
   e. Theodore Roosevelt

4. The "silver issue"
   a. had little support from Democrat William Jennings Bryan
   b. divided the Republican Party during the 1892 election
   *c. refers to the fight to increase the money supply by minting silver money
   d. had dissipated from American politics by the 1896 election
   e. all of the above

5. Which statement about the 1896 election is false?
   a. William McKinley's victory ended the political stalemate that had persisted since 1876
   b. The Populist Party declined after the election
   c. The election is considered the first modern presidential campaign
   d. William McKinley's campaign raised millions of dollars compared to William Jennings Bryan's coffer that was less than $500,000
   *e. William Jennings Bryan lost because the Populist Party's candidate took votes away from Bryan

6. Which institution was hardest hit by the "Redeemers" once they assumed power in the South?
   a. churches
   *b. public schools
   c. mental health facilities
   d. jails
   e. sharecropping

7. Which statement about the disenfranchisement of blacks in the South is false?
   a. Some states saw coalitions between black Republicans and anti-Redeemer Democrats to prevent the disenfranchisement of blacks
   b. Between 1890 and 1906, every southern state enacted laws or constitutional provisions meant to eliminate the black vote
   c. In passing various laws to restrict blacks from voting, numerous poor and illiterate whites also lost the right to vote in the South
   d. The elimination of black and many white voters could not have been accomplished without the approval of the North
   *e. The Supreme Court refused to invalidate the grandfather clause for violating the Fifteenth Amendment

8. *Plessy v. Ferguson*
   a. was a unanimous decision
   *b. sanctioned racial segregation
   c. voided the Thirteenth Amendment
   d. limited the hours that women could legally work
   e. was fully supported by Booker T. Washington

9. What was used by southern whites to maintain domination over blacks?
   a. racial segregation
   b. disenfranchisement
   c. unequal economic status
   d. inferior education
   *e. all of the above

10. The difference between "old" and "new" immigrants was
    a. their reasons for migrating to the United States
    b. that the native language for the new immigrants was typically English
    *c. that the new immigrants were from southern and eastern Europe
    d. that old immigrants only came before the Civil War
    e. the median age of the immigrants

11. The Immigration Restriction League called for reducing immigration by
    a. barring prostitutes
    b. excluding the Chinese
    c. limiting immigration via a quota system

    d. allowing only families to enter, not single men

 *e. barring the illiterate

12. A reason behind the passage of the "Chinese Exclusion Act" in 1882 was

    a. the Chinese emperor agreed to it in a "Gentlemen's Agreement"

 *b. a severe recession in the 1870s built up sentiment for it

    c. to recruit for labor to build the transcontinental railroads

    d. the Salvation Army pushed for it as a solution to end prostitution in California

    e. immense political pressure from the American Federation of Labor to do so

13. The Supreme Court decision *United States v. Wong Kim Ark* ruled that

 *a. the Fourteenth Amendment gave Asians born in the United States citizenship

    b. San Francisco had to grant licenses to Chinese-operated laundries

    c. Chinese merchants were exempt from the Chinese Exclusion Act

    d. the federal government had the right to expel Chinese aliens without due process of law

    e. Chinese women were forbidden to immigrate to the United States

14. Booker T. Washington

    a. called for political independence, activism, and higher education

 *b. was an astute leader who appealed to whites with a policy of accommodation

    c. was the first slide trombonist and brought his jazz music up north to Chicago

    d. was born in Massachusetts and received his Ph.D. from Harvard

    e. was arrested for not giving up his seat on a Louisiana passenger rail car

15. How did Samuel Gompers use the idea of "freedom of contract"?

 *a. He used it as an argument against judges' interfering with workers' right to organize unions

    b. He used it to argue for the right of workers to sabotage equipment when mistreated by bosses

    c. He used it to argue for fair contracts between labor and their employers

    d. He used it as a means to justify why the AFL excluded women and blacks from its ranks

    e. He used it to explain the relationship between union members and their president, arguing that the members had a right to replace their president when he abused his powers

16. The Women's Christian Temperance Union (WCTU)

    a. was a small organization of radical feminists

    b. was led by Elizabeth Cady Stanton

 *c. argued that politics was the place for women

   d. was a single issue organization out to ban alcohol
   e. all of the above

17. Alfred Thayer Mahan argued that
   a. God had groomed the Anglo-Saxon race to spread its culture and progress throughout the world
   b. for settlement in the West to take hold, the native Americans had to be removed to reservations
   c. the frontier past best explained the distinctive history of the United States
   *d. for the United States to be a great power, it was imperative that it build a strong navy
   e. it was unwise for the United States to annex the Philippines

18. Journalists who worked for newspapers like William Randolph Hearst's *New York Journal* and sensationalized events to sell papers were called
   *a. yellow journalists
   b. trustees
   c. social reformers
   d. muckrakers
   e. freelancers

19. Which statement about the Spanish-American War is true?
   *a. The war lasted only four months and resulted in less than four hundred battle casualties
   b. Congress indicated through the Platt Amendment that it was not going to war to annex Cuba
   c. The war came as little surprise given the fact William McKinley campaigned in 1896 on a platform favoring imperial expansion
   d. Admiral Dewey secured Manila Bay by defeating the Spanish in a bloody three-day battle
   e. The treaty that ended the war granted U.S. citizenship to the peoples of the Philippines, Puerto Rico, and Guam

20. What stated that the Constitution did not fully apply to the territories recently acquired by the United States?
   a. Teller Amendment
   *b. Insular Cases
   c. Platt Amendment
   d. Foraker Act
   e. Exclusion Act

## True or False

T    1. The Homestead Strike demonstrated that neither a powerful union nor public opinion could influence the conduct of the largest corporations.

T    2. The Populists made remarkable efforts to unite black and white small farmers on a common political and economic program.

F    3. The Populists made determined efforts to appeal to industrial workers and ultimately succeed in getting labor's support.

T    4. Some view L. Frank Baum's book, *The Wonderful Wizard of Oz,* as a commentary on the election of 1896 and its aftermath.

T    5. After the 1896 election, voter participation began a steady downhill trend that continues to this day.

F    6. Blacks owned more land in 1900 than they did at the end of Reconstruction.

F    7. In a great exodus, African-Americans migrated to California, seeking political equality, freedom from violence, access to education, and economic opportunity.

T    8. In the landmark decision in *Plessy v. Ferguson* (1896), the Supreme Court gave its approval to state laws requiring separate facilities for blacks and whites.

F    9. Education flourished in the South, with approximately one black high school for each county by 1900.

F    10. Three and a half million immigrants, mostly from northern and western Europe, arrived in the 1890s.

F    11. New immigrants were welcomed and treated with respect because their labor was desperately needed in the cities.

T    12. Chinese demands for equal rights forced the Supreme Court to define the reach of the Fourteenth Amendment.

F    13. Booker T. Washington urged blacks to try to combat segregation and become active in political affairs.

F    14. The American Federation of Labor was very much like the Knights of Labor.

T    15. Through a network of women's clubs, temperance associations, and social reform organizations, women exerted a growing influence on public affairs.

T    16. The depression that began in 1893 heightened the belief that a more aggressive foreign policy was necessary to stimulate American exports.

F    17. America's interest in its new possessions had to do with wanting wealth from natural resources and large-scale American settlement.

F    18. In 1880, the United States was a first-rate power.

T    19. Puerto Rico is the "world's oldest colony" as a commonwealth of the United States.

T    20. Brooks Adams's book *The New Empire* (1902) predicted that because of its economic power, the United States would soon "outweigh any single empire, if not all empires combined."

## Short Answer

*Identify and give the historical significance of each of the following terms, events, and people in a paragraph or two.*

1. Booker T. Washington
2. Populist Party
3. nativism
4. Insular Acts
5. Spanish-American War

6. Homestead Strike
7. black suffrage
8. Chinese Exclusion Act
9. American Federation of Labor
10. lynching

## Essay Questions

1. The strife at Homestead reflected broader battles over American freedom during the 1890s. Defend this statement.

2. Explain why Americans increasingly came to feel that they were being denied economic independence and democratic self-government during the late nineteenth century.

3. How did the Populists seek to rethink the relationship between freedom and government to address the crisis of the 1890s? Why was their platform considered radical? How did their platform seek to guarantee freedom?

4. Chronicle the process that developed in the South of chipping away the freedoms granted to blacks during Reconstruction. By 1900, what was the condition of blacks in the South? How did they respond to those conditions?

5. By 1900, who was entitled to fully enjoy the blessings of American liberty? Be sure to include in your answer blacks, women, labor, immigrants, and colonial subjects.

6. George W. Bush commented in his 2001 inaugural address that America had gone out into the world to protect, not to possess; and to defend, not to conquer. Do you agree or disagree with this statement? Give examples to support your position.

7. Analyze the consequences of American rule in Puerto Rico, Cuba, and the Philippines. Did the citizens prosper? Enjoy freedom? Accept American rule?

8. Explain the various debates that the Spanish-American War triggered over the relationship among political democracy, race, and American citizenship. Be sure to include in your answer arguments made by imperialists and those made by the Anti-Imperialist League.

9. It is early April 1898 and you are William Randolph Hearst. Write an editorial on why the United States ought to declare war on Spain.

**CHAPTER 18** | The Progressive Era, 1900–1916

This chapter concentrates on the history of the Progressive Era, an age when political and economic freedoms expanded for many. The tragic 1911 fire at the Triangle Shirtwaist Company demonstrated the prevailing feeling in America that the government had to be more responsible for the well-being of its people. The chapter continues with a look at growing urbanization and immigration, muckrakers' responses to these forces, and the emergence of a consumer society that brought a new meaning to freedom—consumer freedom. As industry continued to prosper through Fordism and the principles of scientific management, the promise of abundance encouraged workers to fight for higher wages. Freedom's many meanings are explored next, looking specifically at the Socialist Party, labor unions such as the AFL and Industrial Workers of the World (IWW), civil liberties, and a new feminism. Believing that economic freedom was the key to true liberation, Charlotte Perkins Gilman is highlighted in *Voices of Freedom*. The politics of progressivism is discussed next. Progressives assumed that the Modern era required a fundamental rethinking of the functions of political authority. Out of this belief came the idea of "effective freedom." Enlarging democracy, governing by experts, and spearheading reform were all characteristic of the era. Finally, the chapter examines each of the progressive presidents. Theodore Roosevelt identified "good" and "bad" trusts and began a federal conservation program. William Howard Taft expanded upon Roosevelt's policies, but lost his reelection campaign to Woodrow Wilson. Wilson continued the trend of increasing federal regulation over the economy and general welfare of the country.

### CHAPTER OUTLINE

I. Triangle Shirtwaist Company fire

II. An Urban Age and a Consumer Society

A. Farms and Cities
  1. For the last time in American history, farms and cities grew together
  2. American agriculture entered what would later be remembered as its "golden age"
  3. The city became the focus of Progressive politics and of a new mass consumer society
    a. New York was the largest
  4. The city captured the imagination of artists, writers, and reformers
B. The Muckrakers
  1. A new generation of journalists writing for mass-circulation national magazines exposed the ills of industrial and urban life
    a. Lincoln Steffens
    b. Ida Tarbell
  2. Major novelists of the era took a similar unsparing approach to social ills
    a. Theodore Dreiser
    b. Upton Sinclair
C. The Immigrant City
  1. Between 1901 and 1914, 13 million immigrants came to the United States
    a. Ellis Island
  2. Asian and Mexican immigrants entered in fewer numbers
D. The Immigrant Quest for Freedom
  1. Progressive-Era immigration formed part of a larger process of worldwide migration set in motion by industrial expansion and the decline of traditional agriculture
  2. Like their nineteenth-century predecessors, the new immigrants arrived imagining the United States as a land of freedom
    a. Some immigrants were "birds of passage," who planned on returning to their homeland
  3. The new immigrants clustered in close-knit "ethnic" neighborhoods
E. Consumer Freedom
  1. The advent of large department stores in central cities, chain stores in urban neighborhoods, and retail mail-order houses for farmers and small town residents made available to consumers throughout the country the vast array of goods now pouring from the nation's factories
  2. Leisure activities also took on the characteristics of mass consumption
    a. Vaudeville
F. The Working Woman
  1. Traditional gender roles were changing dramatically as more and more women were working for wages
    a. Married women were working more
  2. The working woman became a symbol of female emancipation
  3. Charlotte Perkins Gilman claimed that the road to women's freedom lay through the workplace

    4. Battles emerged within immigrant families of all nationalities between parents and their self-consciously "free" children, especially daughters

G. The Rise of Fordism
    1. Henry Ford concentrated on standardizing output and lowering prices of automobiles
    2. Ford revolutionized manufacturing with the moving assembly line
    3. Ford paid his employees five dollars a day so that they could buy his car

H. The Promise of Abundance
    1. Economic abundance would eventually come to define the "American way of life," in which personal fulfillment was to be found through acquiring material goods
    2. The desire for consumer goods led many workers to join unions and fight for higher wages

I. A Living Wage
    1. Earning a living wage came to be viewed as a "natural and absolute" right of citizenship
      a. Father John A. Ryan
    2. Mass consumption came to occupy a central place in descriptions of American society and its future

III. Changing Ideas of Freedom
A. The Varieties of Progressivism
    1. Progressives wished to humanize industrial capitalism
B. Industrial Freedom
    1. Frederick W. Taylor pioneered "scientific management"
      a. Eroded freedom of the skilled workers
    2. White-collar workers also felt a loss of freedom
    3. Many believed that union embodied an essential principle of freedom—the right of people to govern themselves
C. The Socialist Presence
    1. The Socialist Party brought together surviving late-ninteenth-century radicals
    2. Socialism flourished in diverse communities throughout the country
      a. New York
      b. Milwaukee
    3. Eugene Debs was socialism's loudest voice
D. AFL and IWW
    1. The AFL sought to forge closer ties with forward-looking corporate leaders willing to deal with unions as a way to stabilize employee relations
    2. A group of unionists who rejected the AFL's exclusionary policies formed the Industrial Workers of the World (IWW)
      a. William "Big Bill" Haywood

E. The New Immigrants on Strike
  1. Immigrant strikes demonstrated that while ethnic divisions among workers impeded labor solidarity, ethnic cohesiveness could also be a basis of unity
  2. Lawrence strike demonstrated that workers sought not only higher wages but the opportunity to enjoy the finer things of life
  3. New Orleans dockworker strike showed interracial solidarity
  4. Ludlow strike ended soon after many strikers were killed
F. Labor and Civil Liberties
  1. The courts rejected the claims of labor
  2. Like the abolitionists before them, the labor movement, in the name of freedom, demanded the right to assemble, organize, and spread its views
G. The Free Speech Fights
  1. Labor had to fight to get the right to assemble and speak freely
H. The New Feminism
  1. Feminists' forthright attack on traditional rules of sexual behavior added a new dimension to the discussion of personal freedom
  2. Heterodoxy was part of a new radical "bohemia"
  3. The lyrical left made freedom the key to its vision of society
I. The Rise of Personal Freedom
  1. Issues of intimate personal relations previously confined to private discussion blazed forth in popular magazines and public debates
    a. Sigmund Freud
J. The Birth Control Movement
  1. Emma Goldman lectured on sexual freedom and access to birth control
  2. Margaret Sanger placed the issue of birth control at the heart of the new feminism
  3. The birth control issue became a crossroads where the paths of labor radicals, cultural modernists, and feminists intersected

IV. The Politics of Progressivism
  A. Effective Freedom
    1. Progressives assumed that the Modern era required a fundamental rethinking of the functions of political authority
    2. Drawing on the reform programs of the Gilded Age and the example of European legislation, Progressives sought to reinvigorate the idea of an activist, socially conscious government
    3. Progressives could reject the traditional assumption that powerful government posed a threat to freedom because their understanding of freedom was itself in flux
      a. John Dewey
  B. Progressive Politics
    1. State and local governments enacted most of the era's reform measures

2. Gilded Age mayors Hazen Pingree and Samuel "Golden Rule" Jones pioneered urban progressivism
3. The most influential Progressive administration at the state level was that of Robert M. La Follette, who made Wisconsin a "laboratory for democracy"

C. Progressive Democracy
1. Progressives hoped to reinvigorate democracy by restoring political power to the citizenry and civic harmony to a divided society
2. But the Progressive Era also witnessed numerous restrictions on democratic participation
   a. Voting was seen more as a privilege for a select few

D. Government by Expert
1. The impulse toward order, efficiency, and centralized management was an important theme of Progressive reform
   a. "Mastery" required applying scientific inquiry to modern social problems

E. Spearheads for Reform
1. Organized women reformers spoke for the more democratic side of Progressivism
2. Jane Addams founded Hull House in Chicago
3. The "new woman" was college-educated, middle-class and devoted to providing social services
4. Settlement houses produced many female reformers

F. The Campaign for Suffrage
1. Campaign for women's suffrage became a mass movement
2. By 1900, over half the states allowed women to vote in local elections dealing with school issues

G. Materialist Reform
1. Ironically, the desire to exalt women's role within the home did much to inspire the reinvigoration of the suffrage movement
2. *Muller v. Oregon* upheld the constitutionality of an Oregon law setting maximum working hours for women
   a. Louis Brandeis
   b. A breach in liberty of contract doctrine

H. The Idea of Economic Citizenship
1. Brandeis argued that the right to government assistance derived from citizenship itself

V. The Progressive Presidents
1. The process of nationalization was occurring throughout American life

A. Theodore Roosevelt
1. Roosevelt regarded the president as "the steward of the public welfare"

  2. The Square Deal attempted to confront the problems caused by economic consolidation by distinguishing between "good" and "bad" corporations
 B. Roosevelt and the Trusts
  1. Roosevelt used the Sherman Antitrust Act to dissolve Northern Securities Company
  2. Roosevelt helped mine workers during a 1902 coal strike
  3. Roosevelt improved the Interstate Commerce Commission (ICC) and regulated the food and drug industry
 C. The Conservation Movement
  1. Roosevelt also moved to preserve parts of the natural environment from economic exploitation
   a. John Muir and the Sierra Club
  2. Conservation also reflected the Progressive thrust toward efficiency and control
 D. Taft in Office
  1. Taft pursued antitrust policy even more aggressively than Roosevelt
  2. Taft supported the Sixteenth Amendment to the Constitution
  3. Progressive Republicans broke from Taft after the Ballinger-Pinchot affair
 E. The Election of 1912
  1. The election was a four-way contest among Taft, Roosevelt, Democrat Woodrow Wilson, and Socialist Eugene V. Debs
   a. It became a national debate on the relationship between political and economic freedom in the age of big business
 F. New Freedom and New Nationalism
  1. Wilson insisted that democracy must be reinvigorated by restoring market competition and freeing government from domination by big business
  2. Roosevelt called for heavy taxes on personal and corporate fortunes and federal regulation of industries including railroads, mining, and oil
  3. The Progressive Party platform offered numerous proposals to promote social justice
 G. Wilson's First Term
  1. Wilson proved himself a strong executive leader
  2. With Democrats in control of Congress, Wilson moved aggressively to implement his version of Progressivism
   a. Underwood Tariff
   b. Clayton Act
  3. Wilson abandoned the idea of aggressive trust-busting in favor of greater government supervision of the economy
   a. Federal Reserve system
   b. Federal Trade Commission

## SUGGESTED DISCUSSION QUESTIONS

- How did Progressivism operate in theory and in practice?
- What were the limits of Progressive reform?
- Discuss how working empowered women in the Progressive era. Be sure to comment on the *Voices of Freedom* box.
- How did labor strife bring new meaning to the idea of "freedom of expression"?
- Explain new feminism and why the birth control movement was so radical.
- What were the differences between Roosevelt's New Nationalism and Wilson's New Freedom?

## SUPPLEMENTAL WEB AND VISUAL RESOURCES

Henry Ford
*www.films.com/Films_Home/item.cfm?s=1&bin=1753*
This site contains a brief video biography on Henry Ford as part of a series called "Against the Odds".

Upton Sinclair
*www.kirjasto.sci.fi/sinclair.htm*
This site contains a biography of Upton Sinclair, the writer who is considered to have changed the course of the meatpacking industry.

Fredrick Taylor
*www.cohums.ohio-state.edu/history/courses/hist563/fwt5-29.htm*
This Ohio State University site presents essays and other works from Fredrick Taylor as well as his revolutionary theory of Scientific Management.

Eugene Debs
*1912.history.ohio-state.edu/debs.htm*
Eugene Debs, a loud voice of Socialism in the early 1900s, is the focus here, with links to other relevant material on the subject of Socialism.

Woodrow Wilson
*www.pbs.org/wgbh/amex/wilson/*
This PBS site includes the film *Woodrow Wilson,* from the "American Experience" series.

## SUPPLEMENTAL PRINT RESOURCES

Addams, Jane. *Twenty Years at Hull House.* New York: Penguin, 1998.
Blum, John Morton. *The Progressive Presidents.* New York: W. W. Norton & Company, 1982.

Dorsey, Kurkpatrick. *The Dawn of Conservation Diplomacy: U.S.–Canadian Wildlife Protection Treaties in the Progressive Era.* Seattle: University of Washington Press, 1998.

Gould, Lewis. *America in the Progressive Era, 18901914.* New York: Longman, 2001.

Hoganson, Kristin. "Cosmopolitan Domesticity: Importing the American Dream, 1865–1920." *The American Historical Review* 107, no. 1, (2002): 55–83.

Link, Arthur. *Woodrow Wilson.* Wheeling, IL: Harlan Davidson, 1979.

Newman, Louise Michele. *White Women's Rights: The Racial Origins of Feminism in the United States.* New York: Oxford University Press, 1999.

## TEST BANK

### Matching

| | | |
|---|---|---|
| e | 1. Jane Addams | a. scientific management |
| g | 2. Henry Ford | b. birth control movement |
| i | 3. Eugene Debs | c. Industrial Workers of the World |
| a | 4. Fredrick Taylor | d. Supreme Court justice |
| f | 5. John Muir | e. Hull House |
| b | 6. Margaret Sanger | f. Sierra Club |
| c | 7. Bill Haywood | g. moving assembly line |
| j | 8. Theodore Roosevelt | h. Wisconsin Progressive |
| h | 9. Robert M. La Follette | i. Socialist leader |
| d | 10. Louis Brandeis | j. Square Deal |

| | | |
|---|---|---|
| c | 1. Sixteenth Amendment | a. radical "bohemia" |
| g | 2. New Freedom | b. direct election of senators |
| f | 3. Fordism | c. graduated income tax |
| a | 4. heterodoxy | d. limited working hours for women |
| h | 5. Settlement House | e. writer or journalist |
| i | 6. Federal Reserve Act | f. mass production and consumption |
| j | 7. New Nationalism | g. Wilson's campaign |
| d | 8. *Muller v. Oregon* | h. aid to immigrants |
| e | 9. muckraker | i. twelve regional banks |
| b | 10. Seventeenth Amendment | j. Roosevelt's campaign |

### Multiple Choice

1. Newspaper and magazine writers, who exposed the ills of industrial and urban life, fueling the Progressive movement, were known as
   a. yellow journalists
   b. trustees

    c. social reformers

*d. muckrakers

    e. freelancers

2. Between 1901 and 1914, _____ million immigrants came to the United States.
    a. 4
    b. 7
    c. 10
    *d. 13
    e. 18

3. "Birds of passage" were
    *a. immigrants who planned on returning to their homeland
    b. single women who worked until they got married
    c. strikebreakers who were sent in by factory owners
    d. stowaways on passenger ships attempting to immigrate to America
    e. immigrants who visited settlement houses for temporary help

4. Charlotte Perkins Gilman claimed that the road to women's freedom
    a. lay through higher education
    b. lay through holding political office
    *c. lay through the workplace
    d. lay through access to birth control
    e. lay through being a wife and mother

5. Fordism is
    a. the practice of paying your workers more than the average national wage
    b. a manufacturing system that uses a moving assembly line
    c. the practice of discriminating against unionization
    *d. an economic system based on mass production and mass consumption
    e. a grassroots political movement which fights against special interests

6. Who pioneered a program that sought to streamline production and boost profits by systematically controlling costs and work practices?
    a. Simon Patten
    *b. Fredrick Taylor
    c. Samuel Gompers
    d. J. P. Morgan
    d. Hazen Pingree

7. What was not a measure advocated by the Socialist Party?
    a. free college education
    b. legislation to improve the condition of laborers
    c. public ownership of railroads
    *d. national health insurance
    e. public ownership of factories

8. Which statement about the 1912 textile strike in Lawrence, Massachusetts, is false?
    a. The strike demonstrated that workers sought the opportunity to enjoy the finer things in life
    b. The strike was in response to a reduction in weekly wages
    *c. The strikers asked the American Federation of Labor for assistance
    d. Children of the striking workers publicly marched up New York's Fifth Avenue
    e. The strike was settled on the workers' terms

9. What Progressive-Era issue became a crossroads where the paths of labor radicals, cultural modernists, and feminists intersected?
    a. trust-busting
    b. the initiative and referendum
    c. women's suffrage
    d. unionism
    *e. birth control

10. A cause not widely championed by Progressives was
    a. regulating industry
    b. women's suffrage
    c. prohibiting alcohol
    *d. civil rights for blacks
    e. reducing the poverty of the cities

11. The Progressive movement drew its strength from
    a. big business
    b. farmers
    *c. middle-class reformers
    d. military leaders
    e. socialists

12. Robert La Follette's Wisconsin Idea
    a. utilized primary elections to select candidates
    b. taxed corporate wealth
    c. regulated railroads and utilities
    d. drew on nonpartisan university faculty
    *e. all of the above

13. Settlement houses
    a. provided an alternative to marriage for the "new women"
    b. built kindergartens for immigrant children
    c. were located in poor neighborhoods
    d. established employment bureaus and health clinics
    *e. all of the above

14. *Muller v. Oregon*
    a. refused to limit work hours for male bakers

    *b. argued that women were too weak to work long hours
    c. outlawed child labor for children under the age of sixteen
    d. gave labor the right to strike
    e. validated the liberty of contract

15. Who used the Sherman Antitrust Act to dissolve J. P. Morgan's Northern Securities Company?
    *a. Theodore Roosevelt
    b. Robert La Follette
    c. William Howard Taft
    d. Louis Brandeis
    e. Woodrow Wilson

16. The writer whose work encouraged the passage of the Meat Inspection Act was
    a. Henry George
    b. Theodore Dreiser
    *c. Upton Sinclair
    d. Ida Tarbell
    e. Lincoln Steffens

17. The Sixteenth Amendment
    a. called for the direct election of Senators
    *b. authorized Congress to implement a graduated income tax
    c. granted women the right to vote
    d. prohibited the use and sale of alcohol
    e. instituted the initiative, referendum, and recall

18. Who was not a candidate in the 1912 presidential election?
    a. Theodore Roosevelt
    b. Woodrow Wilson
    c. Eugene Debs
    *d. William Jennings Bryan
    e. William Howard Taft

19. The main difference between New Nationalism and New Freedom was
    a. over civil rights for blacks
    b. over women's place in the public sphere
    *c. over regulating versus trust-busting
    d. over the issue of free silver
    e. over immigration restrictions versus an open gate

20. A frank acceptance of the benefits of bigness, coupled with the intervention of government to counteract its abuses best describes the philosophy behind
    a. socialism
    b. New Freedom
    c. Populism
    *d. New Nationalism
    e. New Deal

**True or False**

F    1. The doors were locked at the Triangle Shirtwaist Company the day of the fire because the manager tragically forgot to unlock them when he arrived in the morning.

T    2. Ida Tarbell wrote a piercing two-volume history of the Standard Oil Company.

T    3. Progressive-Era immigration formed part of a larger process of worldwide migration set in motion by industrial expansion and the decline of traditional agriculture.

F    4. Charlotte Perkins Gilman argued that economic independence did not necessarily mean a change in the home and family relationship.

T    5. During the Progressive Era, the working woman became a symbol of female emancipation.

F    6. Henry Ford paid his employees five dollars a day because he wished to avoid strikes at his factory.

T    7. Economic abundance would eventually come to define the "American way of life," in which personal fulfillment was to be found through acquiring material goods.

F    8. Progressives wished to completely change industrial capitalism and move toward socialism.

F    9. Louis Brandeis was an enemy of the labor movement and led the Supreme Court in its many pro-business decisions.

T    10. In 1912, the socialist weekly newspaper *Appeal to Reason* was the largest paper in the country.

F    11. Compared to the American Federation of Labor, the Industrial Workers of the World union was conservative for its day.

T    12. Like the abolitionists before them, the labor movement, in the name of freedom, demanded the right to assemble, organize, and spread its views.

F    13. New sexual attitudes during the Progressive age were limited to the radical bohemia of New York's Greenwich Village.

T    14. Drawing on the reform programs of the Gilded Age and the example of European legislation, Progressives sought to reinvigorate the idea of an activist, socially conscious government.

F    15. The federal government enacted most of the era's reform measures.

T    16. The "new woman" was college-educated, middle-class, and devoted to providing social services.

T    17. The Conservation movement reflected the Progressive thrust toward efficiency and control.

T    18. When Theodore Roosevelt failed to win the Republican nomination for president in 1912 he formed his own political party.

F    19. Theodore Roosevelt was the first president since John Adams to personally deliver his messages to Congress, rather than sending them in written form.

F    20. Once in office, Woodrow Wilson was a fierce trust-buster, dismantling more than a twenty monopolies.

## Short Answer

*Identify and give the historical significance of each of the following terms, events, and people in a paragraph or two.*

1. Robert La Follette
2. Square Deal
3. "new woman"
4. IWW
5. Progressive Party
6. Northern Securities Company
7. New Freedom v. New Nationalism
8. socialism
9. conservationism
10. "effective freedom"

## Essay Questions

1. In what ways did the Progressive Era see the expansion of political and economic freedoms?

2. In what ways did the Progressive Era see the contraction of political and economic freedoms?

3. Explain how it was in Progressive America that the promise of mass consumption became the foundation for a new understanding of freedom, one in which people had access to the cornucopia of goods made available by modern consumption.

4. Thinking back to previous chapters, compare the writings and influence of the Progressive Simon Patten to the Gilded Age social theorists like Henry George and Edward Bellamy. How did each define freedom? How did each view the future of America?

5. Analyze the various roles women played during the era, from social reformer, to feminist, to suffragette. How did various women define freedom? Be sure to distinguish among different types of women and include the *Voices of Freedom* excerpt in your response.

6. Freedom of expression was given new meaning by labor in the Progressive age. Thinking back to previous chapters, compare the various movements to expand the meaning of freedom of expression—from the Alien and Sedition Acts to the abolitionists in the Antebellum Era—with the labor movement in the Progressive age.

7. Compare the Populist and Progressive movements. Critically analyze why the Progressive movement seemed to have more success. What were the limitations of the Populist movement?

8. What did Progressives mean by "effective freedom"? How was this idea applied to Progressive reforms?

9. Compare the presidencies of Roosevelt, Taft, and Wilson. What made them "Progressive" presidents? Identify what you believe to be the most important pieces of legislation passed during each administration. Why are these so significant? Finally, be sure to indicate what each president did to expand the meaning of freedom for Americans.

**CHAPTER 19**

# Safe for Democracy: The United States and World War I, 1916–1920

This chapter concentrates on the history of America during World War I. It opens with a definition of Woodrow Wilson's concept of a moral foreign policy through what he called "liberal internationalism." Promising to bring the Progressive agenda to the world, Wilson fell short and the war forced Americans to once again debate the true extent of liberty. Quickly looking at the foreign policies of Theodore Roosevelt and William Howard Taft, the chapter embarks on the road toward war. Wilson initially took the stance of neutrality, but when he was pushed into war his Fourteen Points outlined for the world his vision that this war should make the world safe for democracy. At home, the war was sold to the American public via the Committee on Public Information. Progressives used the war to expand their agenda, culminating in the Eighteenth and Nineteenth Amendments. However, freedom of speech was not a cause taken up by Progressives as Eugene Debs's powerful statement in *Voices of Freedom* illustrates. The war also forced Americans to define who was an American. "Race" had earned a legitimate place in science through eugenics, which fueled the anti-immigrant sentiment of the era. Anti-German hysteria ran particularly high during the war, as German-Americans were forced to prove their loyalty. Blacks were also asked to work in defense industries and serve in the army, only to face continued discrimination and violence. Asking Wilson to make America safe for democracy, W. E. B. Du Bois emerged as a leader of the black community through his Niagara Movement and NAACP. Seen as an alternative to Du Bois, Marcus Garvey launched a separatist movement. The chapter ends with the events of 1919. In the face of a worldwide revolutionary upsurge, American labor was attacked during the Red Scare as dangerous and part of a communist conspiracy. Finally, Wilson's dreams for the peace were shattered when the United States Senate refused to ratify the Treaty of Versailles.

# CHAPTER OUTLINE

I. American "liberal internationalism"

II. An Era of Intervention
   A. I Took the Canal Zone
      1. Roosevelt was more active in international diplomacy than most of his predecessors
      2. Roosevelt pursued a policy of intervention in Central America
         a. Panama
   B. The Roosevelt Corollary
      1. The United States had the right to exercise "an international police power" in the Western Hemisphere
         a. Venezuela and the Dominican Republic
      2. Taft emphasized economic investment and loans from American banks, rather than direct military intervention
         a. Dollar Diplomacy
   C. Moral Imperialism
      1. Wilson repudiated Dollar Diplomacy and promised a new foreign policy that would respect Latin America's independence
      2. He believed that the export of American manufactured goods and investments went hand in hand with the spread of democratic ideals
      3. Wilson's "moral imperialism" produced more military interventions in Latin America than any president before or since
   D. Wilson and Mexico
      1. The Mexican Revolution began in 1911
      2. When civil war broke out in Mexico, Wilson ordered American troops to land at Vera Cruz
         a. Mexicans greeted the marines as invaders rather than liberators

III. America and the Great War
      1. War broke out in Europe in 1914
      2. The war dealt a severe blow to the optimism and self-confidence of Western civilization
   A. Neutrality and Preparedness
      1. As war engulfed Europe, Americans found themselves sharply divided
      2. Wilson proclaimed American neutrality, but American commerce and shipping were soon swept into the conflict
         a. *Lusitania*
      3. By the end of 1915 Wilson embarked on a policy of "preparedness"
   B. The Road to War
      1. Wilson won reelection in 1916 on the slogan "He Kept Us Out of War"
      2. Wilson called for a "peace without victory," but Germany resumed submarine warfare
      3. Zimmerman Note was intercepted in 1917

C. The Fourteen Points
   1. Russia pulled out of the war after the Lenin Revolution in 1917
   2. Wilson issued the Fourteen Points in January 1918
      a. They established the agenda for the peace conference that followed the war
   3. When American troops finally arrived in Europe, they turned the tide of battle

IV. The War at Home
  A. The Progressives' War
    1. Some Progressives viewed the war as an opportunity to disseminate Progressive values around the globe
    2. The war created a national state with unprecedented powers and a sharply increased presence in Americans' everyday lives
      a. Selective Service Act
      b. War Industries Board
      c. War Labor Board
  B. The Propaganda War
    1. The Wilson administration decided that patriotism was too important to leave to the private sector
    2. The Committee on Public Information (CPI) was created
      a. The CPI's activities set a precedent for active governmental efforts to shape public opinion in later international conflicts
  C. The Great Cause of Freedom
    1. The CPI couched its appeal in the Progressive language of social cooperation and expanded democracy
    2. Freedom took on new significance
  D. The Coming of Women's Suffrage
    1. America's entry into the war threatened to tear apart the suffrage movement
      a. Jeannette Rankin opposed war
    2. The National Woman's Party was militantly fighting for suffrage
      a. Alice Paul
    3. The combined efforts of women during the war won them suffrage
      a. Nineteenth Amendment
  E. Prohibition
    1. Numerous impulses flowed into the renewed campaign to ban intoxicating liquor
    2. Like the suffrage movement, prohibitionists came to see national legislation as their best strategy
      a. War gave them added ammunition
      b. Eighteenth Amendment
  F. Liberty in Wartime
    1. Randolph Bourne predicted that the war would empower not reformers but the "least democratic forces in American life"

    2. The Espionage Act of 1917 prohibited not only spying and interfering with the draft but also "false statements" that might impede military success

    3. Eugene V. Debs was convicted in 1918 under the Espionage Act for delivering an antiwar speech

      a. Debs ran for president while still in prison in 1920

  G. Coercive Patriotism

    1. Attitudes toward the American flag became a test of patriotism

    2. Patriotism now meant support for the government, the war, and the American economic system

    3. The American Protective League (APL) helped the Justice department identify radicals and critics of the war

      a. IWW

        i. Bisbee, Arizona copper miners

V. Who Is an American?

  A. The "Race Problem"

    1. The "race problem" had become a major subject of public concern

    2. Eugenics, which studied the alleged mental characteristics of different races, gave anti-immigrant sentiment an air of professional expertise

  B. Americanization and Pluralism

    1. "Americanization" meant the creation of a more homogenous national culture

      a. Israel Zangwill's *The Melting Pot*

      b. Ford Motor Company's Sociological department

    2. A minority of Progressives questioned Americanization efforts and insisted on respect for immigrant subcultures

      a. Jane Addams's Hull House

      b. Randolph Bourne

  C. Wartime Americanization

    1. Until the United States entered World War I, efforts at assimilation were largely conducted by private organizations

      a. 100 percent Americanism

    2. The Committee on Public Information renamed the Fourth of July, 1918, Loyalty Day

  D. The Anti-German Crusade

    1. German-Americans bore the brunt of forced Americanization

    2. The use of German and expressions of German culture became a target of pro-war organizations

  E. Toward Immigration Restriction

    1. The war strengthened the conviction that certain kinds of undesirable persons ought to be excluded altogether

      a. IQ test introduced in 1916

    2. In 1917, Congress required that immigrants be literate in English or another language

F. Groups Apart

    1. The war led to further growth of the Southwest's Mexican population

    2. On the eve of American entry into World War I, Congress terminated the status "citizen of Puerto Rico" and conferred American citizenship on residents of the island

    3. Even more restrictive were policies toward Asian-Americans

       a. Gentlemen's Agreement of 1907

G. The Color Line

    1. The freedoms of the Progressive Era did not apply to blacks

    2. Progressive intellectuals, social scientists, labor reformers, and suffrage advocates displayed a remarkable indifference to the black condition

H. Roosevelt, Wilson, and Race

    1. Although Roosevelt had invited Booker T. Washington to dine with him at the White House, he still felt blacks were "wholly unfit for the suffrage"

    2. Wilson's administration imposed racial segregation in federal departments in Washington, D.C., and numerous black federal employees

       a. *Birth of a Nation*

I. W. E. B. Du Bois and the Revival of Black Protest

    1. Du Bois tried to reconcile the contradiction between what he called "American freedom for whites and the continuing subjection of Negroes"

       a. *The Souls of Black Folk* (1903)

    2. In some ways, Du Bois was a typical Progressive who believed that investigation, exposure, and education would lead to solutions for social problems

       a. The Niagara movement sought to reinvigorate the abolitionist tradition

          i. The Declaration of Principles

    3. Du Bois was a cofounder of the National Association for the Advancement of Colored People (NAACP)

       a. *Bailey v. Alabama*

J. Closing Ranks

    1. Most black leaders saw American participation in the war as an opportunity to make real the promise of freedom

    2. During World War I, closing ranks did not bring significant gains

K. The Great Migration

    1. The war opened thousands of industrial jobs to black laborers for the first time, inspiring a large-scale migration from South to North

       a. 500,000 migrated north

      2. Many motives sustained the Great Migration
   L. In the Promised Land
      1. Dozens of blacks were killed during a 1917 riot in East St. Louis, Missouri
      2. Violence was not confined to the North
   M. The Rise of Garveyism
      1. Marcus Garvey launched a separatist movement
        a. Freedom for Garveyites meant national self-determination

VI. 1919
      1. There was a worldwide revolutionary upsurge in 1919
   A. Upheaval in America
      1. In the United States, 1919 also witnessed unprecedented turmoil
      2. By the war's end, many Americans believed that the country stood on the verge of what Herbert Hoover called "a new industrial order"
      3. The strike wave began in January 1919 in Seattle
   B. The Great Steel Strike
      1. The wartime rhetoric of economic democracy and freedom helped to inspire the era's greatest labor uprising
        a. Striked for union recognition, higher wages, and an eight-hour day
      2. Steel magnates launched a concerted counterattack
        a. Associated the strikers with the IWW
   C. The Red Scare
      1. This was a short-lived but intense period of political intolerance inspired by the postwar strike wave and the social tensions and fears generated by the Russian Revolution
      2. Attorney General Palmer in November 1919 and January 1920 dispatched federal agents to raid the offices of radical and labor organizations throughout the country
        a. J. Edgar Hoover
      3. Secretary of Labor Louis Post began releasing imprisoned immigrants and the Red Scare collapsed
   D. Wilson at Versailles
      1. The Versailles Treaty did accomplish some of Wilson's goals
      2. The Versailles Treaty was a harsh document that all but guaranteed future conflict in Europe
   E. Impossible Demands
      1. Wilson's language of "self-determination" raised false hopes for many peoples
      2. The British and French had no intention of applying this principle to their own empires
        a. Ottoman Empire and the League of Nations "mandates"
      3. Du Bois concluded that Wilson had "never at any single moment meant to include in his democracy" black Americans or the colonial peoples of the world

F. The Treaty Debate
   1. Wilson viewed the new League of Nations as the war's finest legacy
   2. Opponents viewed the League as a threat to deprive the country of its freedom of action
   3. On its own terms, the war to make the world safe for democracy failed

## SUGGESTED DISCUSSION QUESTIONS

- Explain liberal internationalism.
- When did Teddy Roosevelt use a big stick and when did he speak softly?
- How were immigrants treated during World War I? Why was there so much anti-German sentiment?
- Compare the Alien and Sedition Acts issued during the Quasi War with France with the Sedition Act issued by Wilson during World War I. Be sure to use the *Voices of Freedom* excerpt.
- Discuss the limits of Wilson's extension of democracy. Who was excluded?
- Describe the war experience for African-Americans.
- Discuss the debates surrounding the Treaty of Versailles. Why did the U.S. Senate ultimately reject the treaty?
- Evaluate how successful Wilson was at making sure that World War I was a war fought to ensure a "World Safe for Democracy."

## SUPPLEMENTAL WEB AND VISUAL SOURCES

Panama Canal
   *www.films.com/Films_Home/item.cfm?s=1&bin=8675*
   This video is a detailed study of the production of the Panama Canal in the early part of the twentieth century.

World War I
   *www.lib.byu.edu/~rdh/wwi/*
   Affiliated with the Great War Primary Document Archive, this site is host to many resources for everything military about World War I.

The Red Scare
   *www.boondocksnet.com/gallery/cartoons/reds/*
   This site takes you to the Red Scare of 1919 and gives many examples of related political cartoons.

The Treaty of Versailles
   *www.spartacus.schoolnet.co.uk/FWWversailles.htm*
   This extensive site covers the Versailles Treaty with maps and term definitions to help guide your way through the information.

League of Nations
*www.library.northwestern.edu/govpub/collections/league/background.html*
This site from the Northwestern University Library includes background
information of the League of Nations, its organizational structure, and links to
additional material.

Marcus Garvey
*www.pbs.org/wgbh/amex/garvey/*
This PBS "American Experience" film titled *Marcus Garvey: Look For Me in
the Whirlwind* explores the rise and fall of this remarkable black leader. This
site takes you to the PBS page for Garvey, providing additional information
and teaching materials.

## SUPPLEMENTAL PRINT SOURCES

Baer, Hans. *The Black Spiritual Movement: A Religious Response to Racism.*
 Knoxville: University of Tennessee Press, 2001.
Cooper, Jr., John Milton. *The Warrior and the Priest: Woodrow Wilson and
 Theodore Roosevelt.* Cambridge: Harvard University Press, 1983.
Ellis, Mark. "'Closing Ranks' and 'Seeking Honors': W. E. B. Du Bois in World
 War I." *Journal of American History* 79, no. 1 (1992): 96–124.
Keene, Jennifer. *The United States and the First World War.* New York:
 Longman, 2000.
McKillen, Elizabeth. "Ethnicity, Class, and Wilsonian Internationalism
 Reconsidered." *Diplomatic History* 25, no. 4 (2001): 553–588.
Rosenberg, Emily. *Financial Missionaries to the World: The Politics and Culture
 of Dollar Diplomacy, 1900–1930.* Cambridge: Harvard University Press, 1999.

## TEST BANK

### Matching

| | | |
|---|---|---|
| c | 1. Woodrow Wilson | a. arrested under the Espionage Act |
| f | 2. W. E. B. Du Bois | b. Dollar Diplomacy |
| a | 3. Eugene Debs | c. liberal internationalism |
| h | 4. Alice Paul | d. *The Melting Pot* |
| g | 5. Marcus Garvey | e. first woman member of Congress |
| j | 6. Theodore Roosevelt | f. Niagara Movement |
| i | 7. Randolph Bourne | g. militant black leader |
| e | 8. Jeannette Rankin | h. National Woman's Party |
| b | 9. William Howard Taft | i. "Trans-National America" |
| d | 10. Israel Zangwill | j. Monroe Doctrine corollary |

| | | |
|---|---|---|
| h | 1. Fourteen Points | a. improving the human species by controlling heredity |
| i | 2. CPI | b. relocation of blacks to the North |
| e | 3. Gentlemen's Agreement | c. international police power in Western Hemisphere |
| j | 4. Red Scare | d. a world organization |
| c | 5. Roosevelt Corollary | e. restricted Japanese immigration |
| d | 6. League of Nations | f. IWW |
| b | 7. Great Migration | g. proposed a German-Mexican alliance |
| g | 8. Zimmerman Telegram | h. proposed agenda for the peace conference |
| a | 9. eugenics | i. George Creel |
| f | 10. Wobblies | j. anti-labor crusade after the war |

## Multiple Choice

1. Theodore Roosevelt's taking of the Panama Canal Zone is an example of
   a. his ability to speak softly in diplomatic situations when he knew he was outgunned
   b. international Progressivism, in which the United States was intervening with the sole purpose to "uplift" the peoples of Central America
   c. liberal internationalism, since he worked closely with the French to work out a deal favorable to Panama
   *d. his belief that civilized nations had an obligation to establish order in an unruly world
   e. one of the many wars in which Roosevelt involved the United States

2. What would not be an accurate characterization of America's empire in the early twentieth century?
   a. economic
   *b. territorial
   c. cultural
   d. intellectual
   e. commercial

3. Between 1901 and 1920, U.S. marines landed in Caribbean countries approximately _____ times.
   a. five
   b. ten
   c. fifteen
   *d. twenty
   e. twenty-five

4. What was not a principle of the Fourteen Points?
   *a. an end to colonization

    b. self-determination for all nations

    c. freedom of the seas

    d. open diplomacy

    e. free trade

5. The Fourteen Points attempted to

    a. consolidate political power at home

  *b. provide a peace agenda to create a new democratic order

    c. quiet growing criticism from the Republicans that Wilson was an inept leader

    d. outline the Progressive Party's campaign platform for the 1920 election

    e. organize alliances after the war among fourteen prominent nations

6. Most Progressives came to see the war as a golden opportunity because

    a. they believed that the United States would profit from the war

    b. they supported the socialist ideas of Vladimir Lenin

  *c. they hoped to disseminate Progressive values around the globe

    d. they saw an opportunity to completely restrict immigration

    e. it enabled blacks a chance for economic improvement through defense jobs

7. At the height of World War I, income taxes rose to _____ percent on the wealthiest Americans.

    a. 30

    b. 40

    c. 50

  *d. 60

    e. 70

8. Which group did not support the movement for Prohibition?

    a. urban reformers wishing to undermine the city machines

    b. women reformers who believed men squandered their earnings on alcohol

    c. employers who hoped Prohibition would create a more disciplined labor force

    d. anti-immigrant Protestants who saw temperance as an American value

  *e. Catholics who wished to curb the abuse of alcohol by its parishioners

9. What restricted the freedom of speech by authorizing the arrest of anyone who made "false statements" that might impede military success?

    a. the Alien Act

  *b. the Espionage Act

    c. the War Powers Act

    d. the CPI Act

    e. the Anti-German Act

10. When Eugene Debs was sentenced under the Espionage Act, what did he tell the jury?

    a. that he was happy to serve as a martyr for his cause like John Brown had before him

    b. that Woodrow Wilson was an inept president who ought to be sentenced for sending young men into battle

    c. that as a Socialist he rejected the Constitution of the United States

   *d. that Americans in the past who spoke out against colonialism, slavery, and the Mexican War were not indicted nor charged with treason

    e. that he was not a Communist spy as had been charged and he had been wrongly accused by his political opponents

11. Who fired their employees if they failed to comply with the standards set by the Sociological Department for "Americanization"?

    a. Standard Oil Company

    b. U.S. Steel

    c. American Tobacco Company

    d. Northern Securities

   *e. Ford Motor Company

12. During the war, in what way did Americans react to German-Americans?

    a. In Iowa the governor required that all oral communication take place in English

    b. "Hamburger" was changed to "liberty sandwich"

    c. The director of the Boston Symphony was interned for playing the works of German composers

    d. The teaching of foreign languages was restricted in many states

   *e. All of the above

13. The Gentlemen's Agreement

    a. made Puerto Ricans citizens

   *b. restricted Japanese immigration

    c. allowed Mexicans to cross over to America to take war jobs

    d. promised that labor unions would not strike during the war

    e. forbade German-Americans from registering for the draft

14. Which statement about race and the presidents is false?

    a. Theodore Roosevelt invited Booker T. Washington to the White House

   *b. Theodore Roosevelt believed that blacks were "fit" for soldiering and suffrage

    c. Woodrow Wilson premiered the film *Birth of a Nation* in the White House

    d. Theodore Roosevelt dishonorably discharged black soldiers after an incident in Texas

    e. Woodrow Wilson imposed racial segregation in the federal government

15. Which statement best describes the philosophy of W. E. B. Du Bois?

    a. He believed that blacks had to concentrate on economic freedom by going to school to learn how to become better farmers

*b. He believed that the "talented tenth" of the black community had an obligation to use their education and training to challenge inequality
   c. He believed that over time, white America would come to accept blacks and called for the black community to be patient
   d. He believed that political equality through suffrage was not necessary for the black community to succeed
   e. He believed in a separatist movement, encouraging blacks to move to Liberia

16. Between 1910 and 1920, _____ blacks left the South for jobs in the North and West.
   a. 100,000
   *b. 500,000
   c. 1 million
   d. 2 million
   e. 5 million

17. What did freedom mean to Garveyites?
   a. the vote
   b. education
   c. training
   *d. national self-determination
   e. economic opportunity

18. Which statement about the Red Scare is false?
   a. It was sparked by a worldwide revolutionary upsurge in 1919
   b. The government deported hundreds of immigrant radicals
   c. It propelled J. Edgar Hoover's career as an anticommunist government agent
   *d. It resulted in substantial gains for workers
   e. It all but destroyed the IWW and the Socialist Party

19. The Treaty of Versailles
   a. was a fair and reasonable document given the circumstances
   b. allowed Germany equal participation in the negotiation process
   *c. required Germany to pay over $33 billion in reparations
   d. rejected Wilson's idea for a League of Nations
   e. declared Ireland's independence

20. Senators opposing America's participation in the League of Nations
   a. believed that it was too complicated an organization to join
   *b. argued that it would threaten to deprive the country of its freedom of action
   c. complained that they would only support it if the League was located in New York
   d. were convinced that Great Britain was not going to join, thus making it a weak organization
   e. were ultimately defeated and the United States joined the League in 1921

## True or False

T    1. Theodore Roosevelt was more active in international diplomacy than most of his predecessors.

T    2. The Roosevelt Corollary gave the United States the right to exercise "an international police power" in the Western Hemisphere.

F    3. Woodrow Wilson emphasized economic investment and loans from American banks, rather than direct military intervention, in what was called "Dollar Diplomacy."

F    4. Through his program of "moral imperialism," William Howard Taft produced more military interventions in Latin America than any president before or since.

T    5. Woodrow Wilson issued the Fourteen Points in January 1918, which established the agenda for the peace conference that followed World War I.

T    6. Some Progressives viewed the war as an opportunity to disseminate Progressive values around the globe.

F    7. The combined efforts of women during the war won them suffrage through the Eighteenth Amendment.

T    8. The Espionage Act of 1917 prohibited not only spying and interfering with the draft but also "false statements" that might impede military success.

T    9. Patriotism during World War I meant support for the government, the war, and the American economic system.

F    10. During World War I, most Progressives were outraged at the broad suppression of freedom of expression and spoke out against the Sedition Act.

T    11. Eugenics, which studied the alleged mental characteristics of different races, gave anti-immigrant sentiment an air of professional expertise.

F    12. The war lessened the conviction that certain kinds of persons ought to be excluded from immigrating to America, which had had lots of support before the war.

T    13. Progressive intellectuals, social scientists, labor reformers, and suffrage advocates displayed a remarkable indifference to the black condition in the early twentieth century.

T    14. Although Roosevelt had invited Booker T. Washington to dine with him at the White House, he still felt blacks were "wholly unfit for the suffrage."

F    15. In some ways, Booker T. Washington was a typical Progressive who believed that investigation, exposure, and education would lead to solutions for social problems.

F    16. World War I opened thousands of industrial jobs to black laborers for the first time, inspiring a large-scale migration from South to North called the Great Movement.

T    17. Marcus Garvey launched a separatist movement, encouraging blacks to embrace their African heritage.

T    18. The Red Scare was a short-lived but intense period of political intolerance inspired by the postwar strike wave and the social tensions and fears generated by the Russian Revolution.

F    19. The Treaty of Versailles that ended World War I was a fair document that all but guaranteed future peace in Europe.

T    20. W. E. B. Du Bois concluded that President Wilson had never at any single moment meant to include in his democracy black Americans or the colonial peoples of the world.

## Short Answer

*Identify and give the historical significance of each of the following terms, events, and people in a paragraph or two.*

1. Red Scare
2. Nineteenth Amendment
3. eugenics
4. liberal internationalism
5. Committee on Public Information
6. Niagara Movement
7. Fourteen Points
8. Panama Canal
9. 100 percent Americanism
10. Sedition Act

## Essay Questions

1. Analyze how accurate W. T. Stead was when he argued in *The Americanization of the World: or, the Trend of the Twentieth Century* that the source of American power was located not in military might or territorial acquisition, but in its single-minded commitment to the pursuit of wealth and the relentless international spread of American culture.

2. Explain how Americans used the language of freedom when discussing foreign policy. Analyze the foreign policies of Roosevelt, Taft, and Wilson in your answer. Did the meaning of freedom change with each administration, or stay constant?

3. It is April 1917 and you are a member of Congress and President Wilson wants a declaration of war. Justify your vote for or against war with Germany.

4. Fully discuss and examine the limitations placed upon freedom during World War I. Then compare those circumstances with those during the Civil War. What was the same? What was different? Were restrictions on civil liberties justified in both cases?

5. Analyze why the Progressives would not embrace the cause of civil liberties. Why did they not generally speak out against the broad suppression of freedom of expression during the war?

6. Compare Roosevelt's and Wilson's attitudes toward blacks. How significant were the actions of the federal government in advancing freedoms for blacks during the early twentieth century?

7. Prepare a brief biography on W. E. B. Du Bois. Analyze his arguments and evaluate his success.

8. Progressives continued to make strides during the war. Discuss the various Progressive accomplishments between 1916 and 1920. Comment on why the movement declined by 1920.

9. Explain the various debates surrounding the Treaty of Versailles. Why did the Senate ultimately refuse to ratify the treaty or join the League of Nations?

**CHAPTER 20**

# From Business Culture to Great Depression: The Twenties, 1920–1932

This chapter concentrates on the history of the 1920s. The chapter opens with the Sacco-Vanzetti case, which encapsulated divisions within the larger society. Nativists dwelled on the defendants' immigrant origins. Conservatives insisted that these alien anarchists must die, despite the lack of evidence. By contrast, prominent liberals, such as a future Supreme Court justice Felix Frankfurter and Socialist Eugene Debs, rallied around the convicted men. Despite these divisions, the 1920s was a decade of economic prosperity for many, as the business of America became business. Illustrating the meaning of freedom as linked to prosperity is Andre Siegfried's *Atlantic Monthly* piece in *Voices of Freedom*. The chapter looks at the decline of labor, the shift in the women's movement after the Nineteenth Amendment, and the predominance of the Republican Party overseeing business prosperity and economic diplomacy. The birth of civil liberties is explored next, discussing Hollywood, the American Civil Liberties Union (ACLU), and the Supreme Court. The divisions within society are examined again, within the context of the culture wars. The fundamentalist revolt is seen most vividly through the Scopes trial. In the wake of the anti-immigrant hysteria of World War I, the Ku Klux Klan emerged again, targeting Catholics and Jews, as well as blacks. The anti-immigrant sentiment is capped with the 1924 Immigration Act that strictly limited immigration. On the other hand, cultural pluralism and the Harlem Renaissance celebrated the diversity and pluralism of America. The chapter concludes with the stock market crash of 1929 and Herbert Hoover's attempts at relieving the strains of the Great Depression.

## CHAPTER OUTLINE

I. The Sacco-Vanzetti case

II. The Business of America

A. A Decade of Prosperity
 1. The business of America was business
 2. The automobile was the backbone of economic growth
  a. It stimulated the expansion of steel, rubber and oil production, road construction, and other sectors of the economy
B. A New Society
 1. Consumer goods of all kinds proliferated, marketed by salesmen and advertisers who promoted them as ways of satisfying Americans' psychological desires and everyday needs
 2. Americans spent more and more of their income on leisure activities like vacations, movies, and sporting events
 3. Americans considered their "standard of living" a "sacred acquisition"
C. The Limits of Prosperity
 1. The fruits of increased production were very unequally distributed
 2. Farmers did not share in the prosperity of the decade
  a. California received many displaced farmers
D. The Image of Business
 1. Businessmen like Henry Ford and engineers like Herbert Hoover were cultural heroes
 2. Numerous firms established public relations departments
E. The Decline of Labor
 1. Business appropriated the rhetoric of Americanism and "industrial freedom" as weapons against labor unions
  a. Welfare capitalism
 2. Propaganda campaigns linked unionism and socialism as examples of the sinister influence of foreigners on American life
 3. During the 1920s, labor lost over 2 million members
F. The ERA
 1. The achievement of suffrage in 1920 eliminated the bond of unity among various activists
 2. Alice Paul's National Women's Party proposed the ERA
G. Women's Freedom
 1. Female liberation resurfaced as a lifestyle, the stuff of advertising and mass entertainment
  a. the flapper
 2. Sex became a marketing tool
 3. New freedom for women only lasted while she was single

III. Business and Government
 A. The Retreat from Progressivism
  1. *Public Opinion* and *The Phantom Public* repudiated the Progressive hope of applying "intelligence" to social problems in a mass democracy
   a. "manufacture of consent"

     2. In 1929, the sociologists Robert and Helen Lynd published *Middletown*

     3. Voter turnout declined dramatically

  B. The Republican Era

     1. Government policies reflected the pro-business ethos of the 1920s

       a. lower taxes

       b. higher tariffs

       c. anti-unionism

     2. The Supreme Court remained strongly conservative

       a. Repudiated *Muller v. Oregon*

  C. The Harding Scandals

     1. The Harding administration quickly became one of the most corrupt in American history

     2. Harding surrounded himself with cronies who used their offices for private gain

       a. Teapot Dome scandal

  D. The Election of 1924

     1. Coolidge exemplified Yankee honesty

     2. Robert La Follette ran on a Progressive platform in 1924

  E. Economic Diplomacy

     1. Foreign affairs also reflected the close working relationship between business and government

       a. Washington Naval Arms Conference

     2. Much foreign policy was conducted through private economic relationships rather than governmental action

       a. Bankers loaned Germany large sums of money

     3. The government continued to dispatch soldiers when a change in government in the Caribbean threatened American economic interests

       a. Somoza in Nicaragua

IV. The Birth of Civil Liberties

  A. The "Free Mob"

     1. Wartime repression continued into the 1920s

     2. In 1922, the film industry adopted the Hays Code

     3. Even as Europeans turned in increasing numbers to American popular culture and consumer goods, some came to view the country as a repressive cultural wasteland

  B. A Clear and Present Danger

     1. The ACLU was established in 1920

     2. In its initial decisions the Supreme Court dealt the concept of civil liberties a series of devastating blows

       a. Oliver Wendell Holmes

  C. The Court and Civil Liberties

     1. Holmes and Louis Brandeis began to speak up for freedom of speech

2. The new regard for free speech went beyond political expression
3. Anita Whitney was pardoned by the governor of California on the grounds that freedom of speech was the "indispensable birthright of every free American"

V. The Culture Wars
  A. The Fundamentalist Revolt
    1. Many evangelical Protestants felt threatened by the decline of traditional values and the increased visibility of Catholicism and Judaism because of immigration
    2. Convinced that the literal truth of the Bible formed the basis of Christian belief, fundamentalists launched a campaign to rid Protestant denominations of modernism
      a. Billy Sunday
    3. Much of the press portrayed fundamentalism as a movement of backwoods bigots
    4. Fundamentalists supported prohibition, while others viewed it as a violation of individual freedom
  B. The Scopes Trial
    1. John Scopes was arrested for teaching evolution in school
    2. The Scopes trial reflected the enduring tension between two American definitions of freedom
    3. The renowned labor lawyer Clarence Darrow defended Scopes
      a. Darrow examined William J. Bryan as an "expert" on the Bible
    4. Fundamentalists retreated for many years from battles over public education, preferring to build their own schools and colleges
  C. The Second Klan
    1. Few features of urban life seemed more alien to rural and small-town native-born Protestants than their immigrant populations and cultures
    2. The Klan had been reborn in Atlanta in 1915 after the lynching of Leo Frank, a Jewish factory manager accused of killing a teenage girl
    3. By the mid-1920s it spread to the North and West
  D. Closing the Golden Door
    1. Some new laws redrew the boundary of citizenship to include groups previously outside it
    2. Efforts to restrict immigration made gains when large employers dropped their traditional opposition
    3. In 1924 Congress permanently limited immigration for Europeans and banned it for Asians
    4. To satisfy the demands of large farmers in California who relied heavily on seasonal Mexican labor, the 1924 law established no limits on immigration from the Western Hemisphere
  E. Race and the Law
    1. James J. Davis commented that immigration policy must now rest on a biological definition of the ideal population

      2. The 1924 immigration law also reflected the Progressive desire to improve the "quality" of democratic citizenship and to employ scientific methods to set public policy

  F. Pluralism and Liberty

      1. "Cultural pluralism" described a society that gloried in ethnic diversity rather than attempting to suppress it

         a. Horace Kallen

         b. Franz Boas and Ruth Benedict

      2. The most potent defense of a pluralist vision of American society came from the new immigrants themselves

      3. Immigrant groups asserted the validity of cultural diversity and identified toleration of difference as the essence of American freedom

      4. In landmark decisions, the Supreme Court struck down laws that tried to enforce Americanization

  G. The Emergence of Harlem

      1. The 1920s also witnessed an upsurge of self-consciousness among black Americans, especially in the North's urban ghettos

      2. New York's Harlem gained an international reputation as the "capital" of black America

      3. The Twenties became famous for "slumming"

  H. The Harlem Renaissance

      1. The term "New Negro" in art meant the rejection of established stereotypes and a search for black values to put in their place

         a. Claude McKay

VI. The Great Depression

  A. The Election of 1928

      1. Hoover seemed to exemplify what was widely called the "new era" of American capitalism

      2. Hoover's opponent in 1928 was Alfred E. Smith of New York

      3. Smith's Catholicism became the focus of the race

  B. The Coming of the Depression

      1. On October 21, 1929, Hoover gave a speech that was a tribute to progress, and especially to businessmen and scientists

      2. The stock market crash did not, by itself, cause the Depression

      3. The global financial system was ill-equipped to deal with the crash

      4. In 1932, the economy hit rock bottom

  C. Americans and the Depression

      1. The Depression transformed American life

      2. The image of big business, carefully cultivated during the 1920s, collapsed as congressional investigations revealed massive irregularities among bankers and stockbrokers

      3. Twenty thousand unemployed World War I veterans descended on Washington in the spring of 1932 to demand early payment of a bonus due in 1945

        4. Only the minuscule Communist Party seemed able to give a
           political focus to the anger and despair
    D. Hoover's Response
        1. Businessmen strongly opposed federal aid to the unemployed
        2. Hoover remained committed to "associational action"
        3. Some administration remedies made the economic situation worse
        4. In 1932 Hoover created the Reconstruction Finance Corporation
    E. Freedom in the Modern World
        1. In 1927 freedom was defined as celebrating the unimpeded reign
           of economic enterprise yet tolerating the surveillance of private life
           and individual conscience
        2. By 1932, the seeds had already been planted for a new conception
           of freedom

## SUGGESTED DISCUSSION QUESTIONS

- How did the automobile change American life?
- Debate the merits of the ERA. Why did Alice Paul see it as a logical extension to the Nineteenth Amendment?
- Discuss what the Supreme Court and Congress did during the 1920s to reverse some of the achievements of the Progressive Era. How was freedom used to justify these actions?
- How was the fundamentalist revolt a reaction to the modernization of American society in the 1920s?
- Using the *Voices of Freedom* excerpt, explain how the meaning of freedom was transformed during the 1920s.
- In what ways did blacks express their freedom through the Harlem Renaissance?

## SUPPLEMENTAL WEB AND VISUAL RESOURCES

Pictures
    *memory.loc.gov/ammem/fsowhome.html*
    The Library of Congress has made the American Memory Web site available
    to the public with thousands of pictures dating from the Great Depression to
    the end of World War II.

The Great Depression
    *www.films.com/Films_Home/item.cfm?s=1&bin=9014*
    "Stormy Weather," an ABC news program hosted by Peter Jennings,
    documents the collapse of prosperity in the United States during the Great
    Depression.

The Scopes Trial
*www.law.umkc.edu/faculty/projects/ftrials/scopes/scopes.htm*
Part of the "Famous Trials in American History" series, this site covers every aspect of the Scopes trial debate.

ACLU
*archive.aclu.org/features/f101498a.html*
This site features a movie produced by PBS called *The ACLU — A History.*

The Roaring Twenties
*users.snowcrest.net/jmike/20sdep.html*
This site is an excellent resource for links to relevant information on 1920s America.

## SUPPLEMENTAL PRINT RESOURCES

Clements, Kendrick. *Hoover, Conservation, and Consumerism: Engineering the Good Life.* Lawrence: University of Kansas Press, 2000.
Conkin, Paul. *When All the Gods Trembled: Darwinism, Scopes and American Intellectuals.* Lanham, MD: Rowman & Litttlefield, 1998.
Crunden, Robert. *Body and Soul—The Making of American Modernism: Art, Music and Letters in the Jazz Age, 1919–1926.* New York: Basic Books, 2000.
Ferrell, Robert. *The Presidency of Calvin Coolidge.* Lawrence: University of Kansas Press, 1998.
Galbraith, John Kenneth. *The Great Crash: 1929.* New York: Houghton Mifflin, 1972.
Goldberg, David. *Discontented America: The United States in the 1920s.* Baltimore: Johns Hopkins University Press, 1999.
Martin, Robert. *Hero of the Heartland: Billy Sunday and the Transformation of American Society, 1862–1935.* Bloomington: Indiana University Press, 2002.
Osofsky, Gilbert. *Harlem: The Making of a Ghetto.* Negro New York, 1890–1930, Chicago: Ivan R. Dee, 1996.
Rosenberg, Emily. "Revisiting Dollar Diplomacy: Narratives of Money and Manliness." *Diplomatic History* 22, no. 2 (1998): 155–76.

## TEST BANK

### Matching

| | | | |
|---|---|---|---|
| d | 1. Claude McKay | a. | moving assembly line |
| h | 2. Alfred E. Smith | b. | ERA |
| i | 3. Leo Frank | c. | Teapot Dome scandal |
| j | 4. Oliver Wendell Holmes | d. | Harlem Renaissance |
| c | 5. Warren Harding | e. | *Middletown* |

| | | |
|---|---|---|
| e | 6. Robert and Helen Lynd | f. theory of evolution |
| b | 7. Alice Paul | g. anarchists |
| a | 8. Henry Ford | h. Catholic presidential candidate |
| g | 9. Sacco-Vanzetti | i. Jewish factory manager |
| f | 10. John Scopes | j. Supreme Court justice |

| | | |
|---|---|---|
| d | 1. "New Negro" | a. fundamentalism |
| f | 2. Bonus March | b. discriminated against Catholics and Jews |
| g | 3. Reconstruction Finance Corporation | c. set quotas for immigration |
| i | 4. "slumming" | d. rejection of established stereotypes for blacks |
| h | 5. ACLU | e. reduced navies |
| j | 6. Hays Code | f. unemployed World War I veterans |
| e | 7. Washington Naval Conference | g. government loan agency |
| a | 8. Scopes trial | h. protected civil liberties |
| b | 9. Ku Klux Klan | i. whites seeking exotic adventure |
| c | 10. National Origins Act | j. adopted by film industry |

## Multiple Choice

1. Who was sentenced to death in a controversial criminal trial?
   a. Felix Frankfurter
   b. Eugene Debs
   *c. Nicola Sacco
   d. Clarence Darrow
   e. Leo Frank

2. What did Calvin Coolidge believe was the chief business of the American people?
   a. civil rights
   b. internationalism
   c. spreading liberty
   *d. business
   e. going to church

3. Railroads were to the late nineteenth century what _____ were to the 1920s.
   *a. cars
   b. radios
   c. stock markets
   d. telephones
   e. airplanes

4. Who was not a celebrity of the 1920s?
   a. Charles Lindbergh
   b. Babe Ruth
   *c. Jackie Robinson
   d. Charlie Chaplin
   e. Jack Dempsey

5. Labor unions lost members in the 1920s because of
   a. more open shop businesses
   b. the emergence of welfare capitalism
   c. the tarnished image of labor in the wake of the 1919 labor upsurge
   d. the implementation by corporations of a new style of management, emphasizing human factors in employment
   *e. all of the above

6. For feminist women in the 1920s freedom meant
   a. voting
   b. owning their own property
   c. the ERA
   *d. the right to chose their lifestyle
   e. becoming a wife and mother

7. Which statement about politics in the 1920s is false?
   a. voter turnout had fallen dramatically compared to the turn of the century
   *b. women took an active role in national politics, overwhelmingly supporting the Republican Party
   c. Republicans controlled the White House and supported pro-business policies
   d. the South was dominated by the Democratic Party
   e. Congress continued the trend toward restricting certain groups of people from entering the United States

8. President Harding's call for a "return to normalcy" meant
   a. bringing back the Progressive spirit of reform
   b. demobilizing from World War I
   c. getting women back into the home from their wartime jobs
   *d. a call for the regular order of things, without excessive reform
   e. an end to the radicalism of the Red Scare

9. What is not an example of the economic diplomacy of the 1920s designed to improve American business?
   a. U.S. loans to Germany
   *b. rejecting the League of Nations
   c. Fordney-McCumber tariff
   d. securing access to oil in Venezuela
   e. the Red Line Agreement

10. American novelists like F. Scott Fitzgerald and Ernest Hemingway were part of the
   - *a. Lost Generation
   - b. New Generation
   - c. Me Generation
   - d. Literary Generation
   - e. Greatest Generation

11. The Hays Codes
   - a. barred immigration from Asia
   - *b. outlined inappropriate material for films
   - c. were adopted by corporations to appease unions
   - d. were sanctioned by the ACLU
   - e. raised tariffs to an all-time high

12. The Scopes trial illustrated a divide between
   - *a. modernism and fundamentalism
   - b. Progressives and Democrats
   - c. liberalism and conservativism
   - d. cultural diversity and nativism
   - e. feminism and machismo

13. There were many forces that predisposed potential Ku Klux Klan members to accept its exclusionary message without much analysis. These forces included all of the following except
   - *a. the birth of the Harlem Renaissance
   - b. the 1915 film release of *Birth of a Nation*
   - c. "100 percent Americanism" that developed during World War I
   - d. the 1921 and 1924 Immigration Acts
   - e. rise of fundamentalism

14. The 1924 Immigration Act
   - a. reflected the Progressive desire to improve the "quality" of democratic citizenship and to employ scientific methods to set public policy
   - b. satisfied the demands of large farmers in California who relied heavily on seasonal Mexican labor by not setting limits on immigration from the Western Hemisphere
   - c. Efforts to restrict immigration made gains when large employers dropped their traditional opposition
   - d. permanently limited immigration for Europeans and banned it for Asians
   - *e. all of the above

15. "Cultural pluralism"
   - a. was the adopted philosophy of the Ku Klux Klan
   - *b. described a society that gloried in ethnic diversity

    c. was denounced by Randolph Bourne

    d. described the mood in Congress when it passed the 1924 Immigration
       Act

    e. was the driving force behind the conviction of Sacco and Vanzetti

16. What was considered the "capital" of black America?

    a. Chicago

    b. Detroit

  *c. Harlem

    d. Los Angeles

    e. New Orleans

17. Herbert Hoover

    a. was a mining engineer

    b. was a progressive Republican

    c. was in charge of food relief in Europe during World War I

    d. was well-prepared to be president

  *e. all of the above

18. What issue became the focus of the 1928 presidential race?

    a. the qualifications of Hoover to be president

  *b. the fact that Alfred Smith was Catholic

    c. government regulations on business

    d. immigration policy

    e. what global leadership role America should take

19. The Great Depression was caused by

    a. a land speculation bubble in Florida

    b. an unequal distribution of wealth

    c. an agricultural recession throughout the decade

    d. stagnated sales in the auto and consumer goods industries after
       1926

  *e. all of the above

20. Hoover's response to the Depression was

    a. tax increase

    b. higher tariffs

    c. Reconstruction Finance Corporation

    d. Federal Home Loan Bank System

  *e. all of the above

## True or False

T    1. Europeans rallied in mass protests against the execution of Sacco and
       Vanzetti.

F    2. If one commodity drove the economy in the 1920s, it was the radio.

F    3. Farmers benefited the most from the prosperity of the decade.

T    4. During the 1920s, labor lost over 2 million members.

F    5. Nearly every major female organization supported Alice Paul's National Women's Party's proposal for an Equal Rights Amendment.

T    6. Propaganda campaigns launched by big business linked unionism and socialism as examples of the sinister influence of foreigners on American life during the 1920s.

T    7. Andre Siegfried identified that Americans considered their standard of living a sacred acquisition, which they would defend at any price.

F    8. Calvin Coolidge's administration quickly became one of the most corrupt in American history.

T    9. Foreign policy was largely conducted through private economic relationships rather than governmental action during the 1920s.

T    10. Supreme Court justices Oliver Wendell Holmes and Louis Brandeis began to speak up for freedom of speech in the 1920s.

F    11. The ACLU emerged from the Sacco-Vanzetti trial.

F    12. John Scopes was arrested for teaching the theory of creation in school.

T    13. Fundamentalists supported Prohibition, while others viewed it as a violation of individual freedom.

F    14. The Ku Klux Klan reemerged in the South, targeting only blacks.

T    15. Under the 1924 Immigration Act, no Asians were allowed to immigrate to the United States.

T    16. The term "New Negro" in art meant the rejection of established stereotypes and a search for black values to put in their place.

F    17. The stock market crash caused the Great Depression.

T    18. The Great Depression was global, affecting almost every country in the world.

T    19. The image of big business, carefully cultivated during the 1920s, collapsed as congressional investigations revealed massive irregularities among bankers and stockbrokers.

T    20. Twenty thousand unemployed World War I veterans descended on Washington in the spring of 1932 to demand early payment of a bonus due in 1945.

## Short Answer

*Identify and give the historical significance of each of the following terms, events, and people in a paragraph or two.*

1. Harlem Renaissance
2. 1924 Immigration Act
3. civil liberties
4. Calvin Coolidge
5. Sacco and Vanzetti

6. The Crash
7. fundamentalism
8. Henry Ford
9. Ku Klux Klan
10. Herbert Hoover

## Essay Questions

1. World War I was supposed to be a quick and honorable war. Instead, it was long, bloody, and seemingly void of logic. As such, it dealt a severe blow to the optimism and self-confidence of Western civilization. Give examples that support this statement.

2. Discuss how the Sacco-Vanzetti case laid bare some of the faultlines beneath the surface of American society in the 1920s.

3. Fully discuss what Supreme Court justice Louis Brandeis meant when he argued that freedom to think and speak was "indispensable to the discovery and spread of political truth. . . . The greatest menace to freedom is an inert people."

4. After World War I and more than twenty years of reform, Americans became much more conservative in the 1920s. In fact, Reinhold Niebuhr stated that America was "rapidly becoming the most conservative nation on earth." Give examples that defend this perception of America as "conservative" in the 1920s.

5. One newspaper of the day declared that "the American citizen's first importance to his country is no longer that of a citizen but that of a consumer." Analyze the validity of that statement. Be sure to include in your response a comment on the *Voices of Freedom* excerpt.

6. The two sides of the debates of the Scopes trial defined freedom differently. Explain what freedom meant to each side and how the Scopes trial mirrored the trends in American society during the 1920s.

7. The 1920s is commonly referred to as the "Roaring Twenties." Document who was, and who was not, "roaring" in the 1920s. Your answer ought to illustrate the dichotomy of the decade.

8. The 1920s presents a time when an entire people were grappling with massive technological and social change. Americans spent the decade seeking to adapt

to the rise of a mass-production, mass-culture metropolitan world that had emerged, seemingly overnight. Discuss the decade in these terms, describing the many ways in which Americans sought to deal with this change.

9. The Great Depression came dramatically with the stock market crash, but the causes of the Depression had been planted well before 1929. Discuss what brought on the Great Depression and why Hoover was not able to properly address the crisis.

| The New Deal, 1932–1940

This chapter concentrates on the history of the New Deal era, examining legislation, protest movements, and the impact of the New Deal upon minorities. The chapter opens with the Grand Coulee Dam, a magnificent piece of civil engineering, yet it flooded hundreds of acres of Indian hunting and farming land for which the Native Americans were not compensated. Roosevelt's New Deal accomplished significant achievements, but also had many limitations. The chapter explores the economic recovery programs of the First New Deal and the subsequent wave of protests from men like Upton Sinclair, Huey Long, Father Charles Coughlin, and Dr. Francis Townsend. Pressured by these voices of protest, Roosevelt's Second New Deal focused more on economic security. Labor made remarkable gains during the New Deal, as seen with the establishment of the Congress of Industrial Organizations (CIO). Led by John Lewis, the CIO had a clear vision of what democracy and freedom meant for labor. This understanding is highlighted in his 1936 radio address in *Voices of Freedom*. Roosevelt's "reckoning with liberty" is discussed next, looking at how he gave liberalism its modern meaning as well as his court fight. The limits of the New Deal are then explored, examining the hardships faced by women, Indians, Mexicans, and African-Americans. Finally, the chapter looks at the appeal of the Communist Party during the New Deal and the conservative congressional response to the Popular Front with the establishment of House Un-American Activities Committee (HUAC) and the Smith Act.

## CHAPTER OUTLINE

I. The Columbia River Project

II. The First New Deal
   A. FDR and the Election of 1932
      1. FDR came from a privileged background but served as a symbol for the ordinary man

    2. FDR promised a "new deal" for the American people, but his campaign was vague in explaining how he was going to achieve it

B. The Coming of the New Deal
    1. Conservative and totalitarian leaders led the peoples of Europe in the 1930s
    2. On the other side of the Atlantic, Roosevelt saw his New Deal as an alternative to socialism on the left, Nazism on the right, and the inaction of upholders of unregulated capitalism
    3. FDR relied heavily for advice on a group of intellectuals and social workers who took up key positions in his administration
       a. Secretary of Labor Frances Perkins
       b. Harry Hopkins
       c. Secretary of the Interior Harold Ickes
       d. Justice Louis Brandeis
    4. The presence of these individuals reflected how Roosevelt drew on the reform traditions of the Progressive Era

C. The Banking Crisis
    1. FDR spent much of 1933 trying to reassure the public
    2. Roosevelt declared a "bank holiday," temporarily halting all bank operations, and called Congress into special session
       a. Emergency Banking Act
    3. Further measures also transformed the American financial system
       a. Glass Steagall Act
       b. Federal Deposit Insurance Corporation (FDIC)
       c. Went off the gold standard

D. The NRA
    1. An unprecedented flurry of legislation during the first three months of Roosevelt's administration was a period known as The Hundred Days
    2. The centerpiece of Roosevelt's plan for combating the Depression was the National Industrial Recovery Act
       a. NRA
    3. The NRA reflected how even in its early days, the New Deal reshaped understandings of freedom
       a. Section 7a
    4. Hugh S. Johnson set standards for production, prices, and wages in the textile, steel, mining, and auto industries
       a. the Blue Eagle

E. Government Jobs
    1. The Hundred Days also brought the government into providing relief to those in need
       a. FERA
       b. CCC
       c. PWA
       d. TVA

F. The New Deal and Agriculture
    1. The Agricultural Adjustment Act (AAA) authorized the federal government to try to raise farm prices by setting production quotas for major crops and paying farmers not to plant more
    2. The AAA succeeded in significantly raising farm prices and incomes for large farmers
       a. The policy generally hurt small farms and tenant farmers
    3. The 1930s also witnessed severe drought, creating the Dust Bowl
G. The New Deal and Housing
    1. Home ownership had become a mark of respectability, but the Depression devastated the American housing industry
    2. Hoover's administration established a federally sponsored bank to issue home loans
    3. FDR moved energetically to protect homeowners from foreclosure and to stimulate new construction
       a. Home Owners Loan Corporation
       b. Federal Housing Administration (FHA)
    4. There were other important measures of Roosevelt's first two years in office
       a. Twenty-first Amendment
       b. FCC
       c. SEC
H. The Court and the New Deal
    1. In 1935, the Supreme Court began to invalidate key New Deal laws
       a. NRA
       b. AAA

III. The Grassroots Revolt
A. Labor's Great Upheaval
    1. Previous depressions, like those of the 1870s and 1890s, had devastated the labor movement
    2. A cadre of militant labor leaders provided leadership to the labor upsurge
    3. Workers' demands during the 1930s went beyond better wages
       a. All their goals required union recognition
    4. Roosevelt's election as president did much to rekindle hope among labor
    5. 1934 saw an explosion of strikes
B. The Rise of the CIO
    1. The labor upheaval posed a challenge to the American Federation of Labor
    2. John Lewis led a walkout of the AFL that produced a new labor organization, the Congress of Industrial Organizations (CIO)

       3. The UAW led a sit-down strike in 1936

       4. Steel workers tried to follow suit

       5. Union membership reached 9 million by 1940

   C. Labor and Politics

       1. The labor upsurge altered the balance of economic power and propelled to the forefront of politics labor's goal of a fairer, freer, more equal America

       2. CIO leaders explained the Depression as the result of an imbalance of wealth and income

   D. Voices of Protest

       1. Other popular movements of the mid-1930s also placed the question of economic justice on the political agenda

          a. Upton Sinclair and EPIC

          b. Huey Long and Share Our Wealth

          c. Father Charles Coughlin

          d. Dr. Francis Townsend

IV. The Second New Deal

   A. Launching the Second New Deal

       1. Spurred by the failure of his initial policies to pull the country out of the Depression and the growing popular clamor for greater economic equality, Roosevelt launched the Second New Deal in 1935

          a. The emphasis of the Second New Deal was economic security

       2. A series of measures in 1935 attacked the problem of weak demand and economic inequality head-on

   B. The WPA

       1. Under Harry Hopkins's direction, the WPA changed the physical face of the United States

       2. Perhaps the most famous WPA projects were in the arts

   C. The Wagner Act

       1. The Wagner Act greatly empowered labor

   D. The American Welfare State

       1. The centerpiece of the Second New Deal was the Social Security Act of 1935

          a. The Social Security Act launched the American version of the welfare state

   E. The Social Security System

       1. Roosevelt preferred to fund Social Security by taxes on employers and workers

       2. Social Security emerged as a hybrid of national and local funding, control, and eligibility standards

       3. Social Security represented a dramatic departure from the traditional functions of government

V. A Reckoning with Liberty
  A. FDR and the Idea of Freedom
    1. Roosevelt was a master of political communication and used his fireside chats to great effect
    2. FDR gave the term "liberalism" its modern meaning
  B. The Liberty League
    1. FDR's opponents organized the American Liberty League
    2. As the 1930s progressed, proponents of the New Deal invoked the language of liberty with greater passion
  C. The Election of 1936
    1. Fight for the possession of "the ideal of freedom" emerged as the central issue of the presidential campaign of 1936
    2. Republicans chose Kansas governor Alfred Landon, a former Theodore Roosevelt Progressive
    3. Roosevelt won a landslide reelection
      a. "New Deal coalition"
  D. The Court Fight
    1. FDR proposed to change the face of the Supreme Court for political reasons
    2. The plan aroused cries that the president was an aspiring dictator
    3. The Court's new willingness to accept the New Deal marked a permanent change in judicial policy
  E. The End of the Second New Deal
    1. The Fair Labor Standards Bill banned goods produced by child labor from interstate commerce, set forty cents as the minimum hourly wage, and required overtime pay for hours of work exceeding forty per week
    2. The year 1937 witnessed a sharp downturn of the economy

VI. The Limits of Change
  A. The New Deal and American Women
    1. Eleanor Roosevelt transformed the role of "first lady"
    2. However, organized feminism, already in disarray during the 1920s, disappeared as a political force
    3. Most New Deal programs did not exclude women from benefits but the ideal of the male-headed household powerfully shaped social policy
  B. The Southern Veto
    1. The power of the Solid South helped to mold the New Deal welfare state into an entitlement of white Americans
      a. The Social Security law excluded agricultural and domestic workers, the largest categories of black employment
    2. Political left and black organizations lobbied for changes in Social Security

C. The Stigma of "Welfare"
   1. Blacks became more dependent upon welfare because they were excluded from eligibility for other programs
D. The Indian and Mexican New Deals
   1. Under Commissioner of Indian Affairs John Collier, the administration launched an "Indian New Deal"
   2. It marked the most radical shift in Indian policy in the nation's history
   3. For Mexican-Americans, the Depression was a wrenching experience
E. Last Hired, First Fired
   1. African-Americans were hit hardest by the Depression
   2. The Depression propelled economic survival to the top of the black agenda
F. A New Deal for Blacks
   1. FDR appointed a number of blacks to important federal positions
      a. Mary McLeod Bethune
   2. The 1930s witnessed a historic shift in black voting patterns
      a. Shift to Democratic Party
   3. Federal housing policy revealed the limits of New Deal freedom
   4. Federal employment practices also discriminated on the basis of race
   5. Not until the Great Society of the 1960s would those left out of New Deal programs win inclusion in the American welfare state

VII. A New Conception of America
   A. The Heyday of American Communism
      1. In the mid-1930s, the left enjoyed a shaping influence on the nation's politics and culture
      2. The Communist Party's commitment to socialism resonated with a widespread belief that the Depression had demonstrated the bankruptcy of capitalism
         a. The Popular Front
   B. Redefining the People
      1. The Popular Front vision for American society was that the American Way of Life meant unionism and social citizenship, not the unbridled pursuit of wealth
      2. The "common man," Roosevelt proclaimed, embodied "the heart and soul of our country"
         a. Artists and writers captured the "common man"
      3. The Popular Front forthrightly sought to promote the idea that the country's strength lay in diversity, tolerance, and the rejection of ethnic prejudice and class privilege
      4. Popular Front culture presented a heroic but not uncritical picture of the country's past
         a. Martha Graham
         b. Earl Robinson

C. Challenging the Color Line
   1. Popular Front culture moved well beyond New Deal liberalism in condemning racism as incompatible with true Americanism
   2. The Communist-dominated International Labor Defense mobilized popular support for black defendants victimized by racist criminal justice system
      a. Scottsboro case
   3. The CIO welcomed black members and advocated the passage of antilynching laws and the return of voting rights to southern blacks
D. Labor and Civil Liberties
   1. Another central element of Popular Front public culture was its mobilization for civil liberties, especially the right of labor to organize
   2. Labor militancy helped to produce an important shift in the understanding of civil liberties
   3. In 1939, Attorney General Frank Murphy established a Civil Liberties Unit in the Department of Justice
      a. Civil liberties replaced liberty of contract as the judicial foundation of freedom
   4. To counter, the House of Representatives established an Un-American Activities Committee in 1938 to investigate disloyalty
      a. Smith Act
E. The End of the New Deal
   1. FDR was losing support from southern Democrats
   2. Roosevelt concluded that the enactment of future New Deal measures required a liberalization of the southern Democratic Party
   3. A period of political stalemate followed the congressional election of 1938
F. The New Deal in American History
   1. Given the scope of the economic calamity it tried to counter, the New Deal seemed in many ways quite limited
   2. Yet even as the New Deal receded, its substantial accomplishments remained
   3. One thing the New Deal failed to do was generate prosperity

## SUGGESTED DISCUSSION QUESTIONS

- Evaluate the success of the New Deal. Did it end the Great Depression?
- How did the New Deal create a new meaning for liberalism? What, by 1940, is a "liberal" in America?
- Thinking back to previous chapters, what programs of the New Deal were first suggested by earlier radical groups?

- What did the New Deal do for women? Blacks? Indians? Mexicans? Labor?
- Compare the First New Deal with the Second New Deal. What was the focus of each? Which was more successful?

## SUPPLEMENTAL WEB AND VISUAL RESOURCES

WPA
*www.wpamurals.com/index.htm*
This site focuses on the WPA art but has many resources such as timelines and links to other information about this New Deal project.

Social Security
*www.ssa.gov/history/history.html*
This government site covers the history of Social Security along with chronologies and quizzes.

Fair Labor Standards Act
*www.dol.gov/asp/programs/history/flsa1938.htm*
This Department of Labor Web site has a good history of the Fair Labor Standards Act that helped stabilize a minimum wage.

The Dust Bowl
*www.pbs.org/wgbh/amex/dustbowl/peopleevents/pandeAMEX09.html*
This PBS site has information on a video from the "American Experience" series called *Surviving the Dust Bowl.*

Modern Times
*www.teachwithmovies.org/guides/modern-times.html*
In *Modern Times,* a 1936 classic film, Charlie Chaplin critiques modern capitalism during the Great Depression.

## SUPPLEMENTAL PRINT RESOURCES

Draper, Alan. "The New Southern Labor History Revisited: The Success of the Mine, Mill, and Smelter Workers Union in Birmingham, 1934–1938." *Journal of Southern History* 62, no. 1 (1996): 87–108.

Ekbladh, David. "'Mr. TVA': Grass-Roots Development, David Lilienthal, and the Rise of the Tennessee Valley Authority as a Symbol for U.S. Overseas Development, 1933–1973." *Diplomatic History* 26, no. 3 (2002): 335–74.

Hapke, Laura. *Daughters of the Great Depression: Women, Work, and Fiction in the American 1930s.* Athens: University of Georgia Press, 1995.

Harris, J. William. *Deep Souths: Delta, Piedmont, and Sea Island Society in the Age of Segregation.* Baltimore: Johns Hopkins University Press, 2001.

Houck, Davis. *Rhetoric as Currency: Hoover, Roosevelt, and the Great Depression*. College Station: Texas A&M University Press, 2001.

McElvaine, Robert. *The Great Depression: America 1929–1941*. New York: Times Books, 1984.

Perkins, Frances. *The Roosevelt I Knew*. New York: Viking, 1946.

Sitkoff, Harvard, ed. *Fifty Years Later: The New Deal Evaluated*. New York: Knopf, 1985.

Terkel, Studs. *Hard Times: An Oral History of the Great Depression*. New York: Pantheon, 1986.

## TEST BANK

### Matching

| | | |
|---|---|---|
| f | 1. Frances Perkins | a. end poverty in California |
| c | 2. Harold Ickes | b. black cabinet |
| d | 3. John Lewis | c. Secretary of the Interior |
| a | 4. Upton Sinclair | d. CIO |
| g | 5. Huey Long | e. Commissioner of Indian Affairs |
| i | 6. Franklin Roosevelt | f. Secretary of Labor |
| b | 7. Mary McLeod Bethune | g. "Share Our Wealth" Program |
| j | 8. Eleanor Roosevelt | h. Republican presidential candidate |
| e | 9. John Collier | i. court-packing scheme |
| h | 10. Alfred Landon | j. organized a Marian Anderson concert |


| | | |
|---|---|---|
| g | 1. bank holiday | a. investigated disloyalty |
| e | 2. National Recovery Administration | b. hydro-electric project |
| h | 3. Wagner Act | c. International Labor Defense |
| j | 4. Social Security | d. relief for young men |
| a | 5. House of Representatives Un-American Activities Committee | e. Blue Eagle |
| c | 6. Scottsboro case | f. drought-hit area around Oklahoma and Texas |
| i | 7. Popular Front | g. Roosevelt's first action |
| d | 8. Civilian Conservation Corps | h. recognized labor unions |
| b | 9. Tennessee Valley Authority | i. Communists |
| f | 10. Dust Bowl | j. minimum retirement program |

## Multiple Choice

1. Liberalism during the New Deal came to be understood as
   a. limited government and free market enterprise
   *b. active government to uplift less fortunate members of society
   c. a trust in the government to regulate personal behavior
   d. individual autonomy, limited government, and unregulated capitalism
   e. workers' ownership in the means of production

2. During the 1932 election
   a. Franklin Roosevelt boldly outlined his plans for a New Deal
   b. Herbert Hoover made a late rally and nearly defeated Roosevelt
   c. Franklin Roosevelt played upon his disability to garner public sympathy and to make him seem more like an ordinary man
   *d. Franklin Roosevelt called for a balanced government and criticized Hoover for excessive government spending
   e. Herbert Hoover apologized to the American public for failing them and promised to repeal Prohibition if reelected

3. The first thing that Roosevelt attended to as president was
   a. the housing crisis
   b. the farming crisis
   *c. the banking crisis
   d. the unemployment crisis
   e. the tariff crisis

4. Which statement about the New Deal is true?
   a. The Agricultural Adjustment Act (AAA) helped small tenant farmers like those living in the Dust Bowl
   b. The First New Deal dealt mostly with economic security
   c. The New Deal championed civil rights and actively worked at ending Jim Crow
   d. The Second New Deal dealt mostly with economic recovery
   *e. Social Security was a Second New Deal program

5. What was not a New Deal program?
   a. WPA
   *b. CIO
   c. NRA
   d. CCC
   e. FDIC

6. Roosevelt called _____ an American "birthright," the embodiment of the spirit of "enterprise, of independence, and of . . . freedom."
   a. having a job
   *b. owning a home

    c. the right to vote

    d. democracy

    e. social mobility

7. Which two New Deal programs did the Supreme Court rule unconstitutional?

    a. SEC and PWA

    b. NRA and CCC

    c. Glass-Steagall Act and AAA

    d. Wagner Act and NRA

    *e. AAA and NRA

8. What caused union membership to soar in the 1930s?

    a. worker's militancy

    b. tactical skills of a new generation of leaders

    c. changes in government's attitude toward labor

    d. creation of the CIO

    *e. all of the above

9. What statement best describes Huey Long, Upton Sinclair, and Dr. Francis Townsend?

    *a. They all challenged Roosevelt to move further left of center

    b. They were all supported by the Republican Party

    c. Each was a socialist radical

    d. Despite interesting movements, none of them had much of a following

    e. They all ended up in jail during World War II for having communist sympathies

10. The New Deal concentrated power in the hands of which sector of the government?

    *a. the executive

    b. the legislative

    c. the judicial

    d. local government

    e. state government

11. Which program employed white-collar workers and professionals, including doctors, writers, and artists?

    a. PWA

    b. CCC

    *c. WPA

    d. NYA

    e. NRA

12. Which statement about the Social Security Act is false?

    a. It included aid to families with dependent children

    *b. It was extremely original in concept

    c. Congress dropped from the original bill the provision for national health insurance

    d. It created a system of unemployment insurance

    e. Its coverage excluded most blacks from the program

13. The American Liberty League

    *a. protested FDR's policies

    b. organized to fight for the release of the Scottsboro boys

    c. sought to prevent the black singer Marian Anderson from singing at Constitution Hall

    d. lobbied for the passage of the Lundeen bill

    e. supported FDR's isolationist policies regarding foreign affairs

14. Franklin Roosevelt's plan to pack the Supreme Court

    a. aroused cries from critics that he was an aspiring dictator

    b. was proposed because he feared the Court might invalidate Social Security and the Wagner Act

    c. was rejected by Congress

    d. accomplished his underlying purpose

    *e. all of the above

15. Most historians argue that a recession reoccurred in 1937 because Roosevelt

    *a. cut government spending

    b. increased government spending

    c. raised tariffs in face of European competition

    d. was preoccupied with foreign affairs

    e. enacted a policy following Keynesian economics

16. Which statement about the "Indian New Deal" is false?

    a. It ended the policy of forced assimilation

    b. It allowed Indians cultural autonomy

    *c. It continued the policy of the Dawes Act

    d. It replaced boarding schools with schools on the reservations

    e. It failed to allow reservations access to irrigation waters from the Grand Coulee dam

17. During the New Deal, African-Americans

    a. worked in segregated CCC camps

    b. were mostly excluded from Social Security benefits

    c. were discriminated against by the Federal Housing Administration

    d. failed in getting a federal antilynching law passed

    *e. all of the above

18. What group welcomed black members and advocated the passage of antilynching legislation and the return of voting rights to southern blacks?

    a. the Republican Party

    *b. the Congress of Industrial Organizations

    c. the American Liberty League

    d. the Daughters of the American Revolution

    e. House of Representatives Un-American Activities Committee

19. Fearing the growth of the Communist Party in America, Congress passed what piece of legislation?

    *a. Smith Act

    b. Wagner Act

    c. Civil Liberties Act

    d. Lundeen Act

    e. Popular Front Act

20. What ended the Great Depression?

    a. New Deal programs

    b. the rebound of the stock market

    *c. World War II spending

    d. laissez-faire government

    e. a bailout by J. P. Morgan

## True or False

T    1. The Grand Coulee Dam and New York City's Triborough Bridge were both New Deal projects.

T    2. Very few Americans realized that the president who projected an image of vigorous leadership during the 1930s and World War II was confined to a wheelchair.

F    3. Since Franklin Roosevelt came from a humble background, the public came to easily identify him as a symbol for the ordinary man.

F    4. The administrators that Roosevelt choose for his cabinet reflected the conservative traditions of Coolidge and Hoover.

F    5. Despite the efforts of the Bank Holiday, by 1936 banks were still failing in America.

T    6. The Supreme Court ruled that the AAA was unconstitutional.

T    7. Depressions in the past hurt the labor movement, but labor actually made great strides during the Great Depression.

F    8. John Lewis, president of the American Federation of Labor (AFL) led that union in a more radical direction than Samuel Gompers had before him.

T    9. The tactic used by the United Auto Workers in its attempt to gain bargaining rights with General Motors was the sit-down strike.

F    10. Upton Sinclair campaigned for governor of California on the "Share Our Wealth" program.

T    11. Roosevelt launched the Second New Deal because of the failure of his initial policies to pull the country out of the Depression and because of the growing popular clamor for greater economic equality.

F    12. Roosevelt's reelection in 1936 came as no surprise since the entire business community and most of the national newspapers supported the Democrats.

T    13. The Fair Labor Standards Bill banned goods produced by child labor from interstate commerce, set forty cents as the minimum hourly wage, and required overtime pay for hours of work exceeding forty per week.

F    14. Eleanor Roosevelt was a very typical first lady.

T    15. The power of the Solid South helped to mold the New Deal welfare state into an entitlement of white Americans.

F    16. The Indians who lost land from the flooding of the Grand Coulee Dam were adequately compensated by the federal government as part of the "New Deal for Indians."

F    17. Upset that the Great Depression devastated their community, blacks rejected the New Deal and continued to support Republican candidates.

T    18. The Communist Party's commitment to socialism resonated with a widespread belief that the Depression had demonstrated the bankruptcy of capitalism.

T    19. The CIO welcomed black members and advocated the passage of antilynching laws and the return of voting rights to southern blacks.

T    20. The Smith Act made it a federal crime to teach, advocate, or encourage the overthrow of the government.

## Short Answer

*Identify and give the historical significance of each of the following terms, events, and people in a paragraph or two.*

1. WPA
2. Huey Long
3. Wagner Act
4. Popular Front
5. First Hundred Days
6. Eleanor Roosevelt
7. FDR and race
8. CIO
9. Supreme Court packing
10. Indian New Deal

## Essay Questions

1. Describe how the Columbia River project reflected broader changes in American life and thought during the New Deal of the 1930s.

2. Analyze how FDR oversaw the transformation of the Democratic Party into a coalition of farmers, industrial workers, the reform-minded urban middle class, liberal intellectuals, northern African-Americans, and the white supremacist South.

3. Explain, with examples, how the New Deal altered the role of the national government. Do you think that the United States will ever revert to a system where states are more important than the national government?

4. Choose a "character" in history (for example, a woman, businessman, African-American, socialist, large farmer, tenant farmer, city dweller, union worker and so on). Describe your scenario between the period 1933 and 1938. Is your character a supporter of FDR and the New Deal? What suggestions might your character offer for ending the Depression?

5. Liberalism took on its modern meaning during the New Deal. Discuss what liberalism meant before Roosevelt and what it referred to during the New Deal.

6. What kinds of new meanings did freedom take on during the New Deal? Was Roosevelt correct in stating that the economic security was a political condition of personal freedom? Do Americans believe that today?

7. Compare the experiences of the industrial worker and the tenant farmer, of men and women, and of white Americans and blacks during the New Deal. Be sure to explain what freedoms and liberties were or were not extended to each group.

8. Compare the New Deal reforms with those of the Progressive Era. How did the New Deal reflect the reform traditions of the Progressive Era? Be sure to include in your answer a discussion about Roosevelt's key administrators.

9. Labor made tremendous gains during the New Deal. Discuss how labor benefited from the NRA, Wagner Act, and CIO. Be sure to comment on the *Voices of Freedom* excerpt in your answer.

## CHAPTER 22

# Fighting for the Four Freedoms: World War II, 1941–1945

This chapter concentrates on the history of the Second World War. Freedom springs forth immediately with FDR's 1941 speech on The Four Freedoms, highlighted in the *Voices of Freedom* box. Attempting to give the war an ideological meaning and convince the American public that it had to be prepared, Roosevelt linked the war's meaning with the freedoms that Americans have taken for granted for years. The chapter looks at FDR's foreign policy in Latin America, the road leading up to the European and Pacific wars, and America's reluctance to intervene until Pearl Harbor. The war on the home front is examined. Americans mobilized quickly and business and labor worked to make America an "arsenal of democracy" while the Office of War Information promoted the Four Freedoms to the American public. The intellectual debates about how the postwar world might define freedom are examined through the writings of Henry Luce, Henry Wallace, Friedrich Hayek, and FDR's Economic Bill of Rights. Ethnic minorities' experiences during the war were varied. While Indians and Mexican-Americans had some opportunities, Japanese-Americans were interned for the war, held as criminals without evidence or due process. Blacks saw the war as an opportunity to win two victories—one abroad and one at home. The modern civil rights movement gets its start with the war, particularly through the work of A. Philip Randolph and through the support of the new liberalism. The war ends with the dawn of the atomic age, which introduced a technology that remains controversial to this day. Preparing for the postwar world, meetings at Bretton Woods and Dunbarton Oaks laid the foundation for a new economic order and international political structure.

## CHAPTER OUTLINE

I. Norman Rockwell's Four Freedoms paintings

II. Fighting World War II

A. Good Neighbors
  1. FDR embarked on a number of departures in foreign policy
    a. Soviet Union
    b. Latin America
B. The Road to War
  1. Japan had expanded its reach in Manchuria and China by the mid-1930s
  2. Germany embarked on a campaign to control the entire continent
    a. Benito Mussolini
    b. General Francisco Franco
  3. Although Roosevelt was alarmed, he was tied to the policy of appeasement
    a. Munich conference
C. Isolationism
  1. American businessmen did not wish to give up profitable overseas markets in Germany and Japan
  2. Many Americans were reluctant to get involved in international affairs because of the legacy of World War I
    a. Nye Committee
  3. Congress favored isolationism as seen with various Neutrality Acts
D. War in Europe
  1. Germany invaded Poland on September 1, 1939
    a. Blitzkrieg appeared unstoppable
  2. For nearly two years, Britain stood virtually alone in fighting Germany
    a. Battle of Britain
E. 1940
  1. FDR wished to help Britain, but public opinion limited him
  2. In 1940, breaking with a tradition that dated back to George Washington, Roosevelt announced his candidacy for a third term as president
F. Toward Intervention
  1. Congress passed the Lend Lease Act in 1941 and froze Japanese assets
  2. Interventionists tried to awaken a reluctant country to prepare for war
    a. Freedom House
G. Pearl Harbor
  1. On December 7, 1941, Japanese planes, launched from aircraft carriers, bombed the naval base at Pearl Harbor in Hawaii
  2. FDR asked for a declaration of war against Japan
H. The War in the Pacific
  1. The first few months of American involvement witnessed an unbroken string of military disasters
  2. The tide turned with the battles at Coral Sea and Midway in May and June 1942

I. The War in Europe
  1. The war in Europe was first fought in North Africa and Italy
  2. D-Day established the much-needed second front in western Europe
  3. The crucial fighting in Europe took place on the eastern front between Germany and the Soviet Union
     a. Stalingrad marked the turning point
  4. The war claimed millions of lives
     a. Holocaust

III. The Home Front
  A. Mobilizing the War
    1. World War II transformed the role of the national government
    2. The government built housing for war workers and forced civilian industries to retool for war production
  B. Business and War
    1. Roosevelt offered incentives to spur production—low-interest loans, tax concessions, contracts with guaranteed profits
    2. The West Coast emerged as a focus of military-industrial production
       a. Nearly 2 million Americans moved to California for jobs in defense-related industries
    3. Americans produced an astonishing amount of wartime goods and utilized science and technology
  C. Labor in Wartime
    1. Organized labor entered a three-sided arrangement with government and business that allowed union membership to soar to unprecedented levels
    2. Unions became firmly established in many sectors of the economy during World War II
  D. Fighting for the Four Freedoms
    1. To Roosevelt, the Four Freedoms expressed deeply held American values worthy of being spread worldwide
  E. Freedom from Want
    1. Roosevelt initially meant it to refer to the elimination of barriers to international trade
       a. It came to mean protecting the standard of living so that it would not fall after the war
       b. Carlos Bulosan
  F. The OWI
    1. Political division generated by the New Deal affected efforts to promote the Four Freedoms
       a. OWI wished to give the war an ideological meaning
    2. Concerned that the OWI was devoting as much time to promoting New Deal social programs as to the war effort, Congress eliminated most of its funding

G. The Fifth Freedom
   1. The war witnessed a burst of messages marketing advertisers'
      definition of freedom
      a. "Free enterprise"
H. Women at War
   1. In 1944 women made up over one-third of the civilian labor force
   2. New opportunities opened up for married women and mothers
I. The World of Tomorrow
   1. Women's work during the war was viewed by men and the government
      as temporary
   2. The advertisers' "world of tomorrow" rested on a vision of
      family-centered prosperity

IV. Visions of Postwar Freedom
   A. Toward an American Century
      1. Henry Luce insisted that the United States embrace a leadership role in
         his 1941 book *The American Century*
         a. Luce emphasized American leadership through active agency, not
            simply by example
      2. Henry Wallace offered a less imperialistic alternative
      3. Luce and Wallace both spoke the language of freedom
   B. The Way of Life of Free Men
      1. The National Resources Planning Board offered a blueprint for a
         peacetime economy based on:
         a. Full employment
         b. An expanded welfare state
         c. A widely shared American Standard of Living
      2. The reports continued a shift in liberals' outlook that dated from the
         late 1930s
         a. Keynesianism
   C. An Economic Bill of Rights
      1. FDR called for an "Economic Bill of Rights" in 1944
      2. The Servicemen's Readjustment Act, or GI Bill of Rights, was one
         of the most far-reaching pieces of social legislation in American
         history
      3. During 1945, unions, civil rights organizations, and religious groups
         urged Congress to enact the Full Employment Bill
   D. The Road to Serfdom
      1. The failure of the Full Employment Bill revealed the renewed
         intellectual respectability of fears that economic planning represented
         a threat to liberty
         a. Hayek's *The Road to Serfdom*
            i. Offered a new intellectual justification for opponents of active
               government

b. Hayek helped lay the foundation for the rise of modern conservatism

V. The American Dilemma
  A. Patriotic Assimilation
     1. The Second World War created a vast melting pot, especially for European immigrants and their children
        a. Roosevelt promoted pluralism as the only source of harmony in a diverse society
     2. Government and private agencies eagerly promoted group equality as the definition of Americanism and a counterpoint to Nazism
     3. By the war's end, racism and nativism had been stripped of intellectual respectability
        a. Ruth Benedict and Ashley Montagu
     4. Hollywood, too, did its part
     5. Intolerance hardly disappeared from American life
  B. Mexican-Americans, Indians, and the War
     1. The war had a far more ambiguous meaning for non-white groups than for whites
     2. The Bracero program allowed tens of thousands of contract laborers to cross into the United States to take up jobs as domestic and agricultural workers
        a. A new "Chicano" culture—a fusion of Mexican heritage and American experience, was being born
        b. "Zoot suit" riots
     3. American Indians served in the army
        a. "Code talkers"
  C. Asian-Americans in Wartime
     1. Asian-Americans' war experience was filled with paradox
     2. Chinese exclusion was abolished
     3. Japanese were viewed by Americans as a detested foe
     4. The American government viewed every person of Japanese ethnicity as a potential spy
  D. Japanese-American Internment
     1. The military persuaded FDR to issue Executive Order 9066
     2. Internment revealed how easily war can undermine basic freedoms
        a. Hardly anyone spoke out against internment
        b. The courts refused to intervene
           i. *Korematsu v. U.S.*
     3. The government marketed war bonds to the internees and drafted them into the army
  E. Blacks and the War
     1. The wartime message of freedom portended a major transformation in the status of blacks

    2. The war spurred a movement of black population from the rural South to the cities of the North and West

       a. Detroit race riot

  F. Blacks and the Military

    1. During the war, over 1 million blacks served in the armed forces

    2. Black soldiers sometimes had to give up their seats on railroad cars to accommodate Nazi prisoners of war

  G. Birth of the Civil Rights Movement

    1. The war years witnessed the birth of the modern civil rights movement

    2. The black labor leader A. Philip Randolph called for a march on Washington in July 1941

       a. Executive Order 8802 and FEPC

    3. Although the FEPC lacked enforcement powers, it marked a significant shift in public policy

  H. The Double-V

    1. The "double-V" meant that victory over Germany and Japan must be accompanied by victory over segregation at home

  I. What the Negro Wants

    1. During the war, a broad political coalition centered on the left but, reaching well beyond it, called for an end to racial inequality in America

    2. CIO unions made significant efforts to organize black workers and win them access to skilled positions

    3. The new black militancy created a crisis for moderate white southerners

       a. *What the Negro Wants*

    4. The South reacted to preserve white supremacy

  J. Toward Racial Liberalism

    1. The status of black Americans assumed a place at the forefront of enlightened liberalism

    2. Wendell Willkie's *One World* attacked "our imperialisms at home"

  K. An American Dilemma

    1. *An American Dilemma* was a sprawling account of the country's racial past, present, and future

       a. Gunnar Myrdal

    2. Myrdal noted the conflict between American values and American racial policies

       a. America had to outlaw discrimination

    3. By 1945, support for racial justice had finally taken its place on the liberal-left agenda alongside full employment, civil liberties, and the expansion of the New Deal welfare state

VI. The End of the War

  A. The Most Terrible Weapon

    1. One of the most momentous decisions ever confronted by an American president fell to Harry Truman

2. The bomb was a practical realization of the theory of relativity
3. The Manhattan Project developed an atomic bomb
B. The Dawn of the Atomic Age
   1. On August 6, 1945, an American plane dropped an atomic bomb that detonated over Hiroshima, Japan
   2. Because of the enormous cost in civilian lives, the use of the bomb remains controversial
   3. The dropping of the atomic bombs was the logical culmination of the way World War II had been fought
C. Planning the Postwar World
   1. Even as the war raged, a series of meetings among Allied leaders formulated plans for the postwar world
      a. Tehran
      b. Yalta
      c. Potsdam
D. A New Economic Order
   1. The Bretton Woods meeting established a new international economic system
E. The UN
   1. The Dumbarton Oaks meeting established the structure of the United Nations
      a. General Assembly
      b. Security Council
   2. World War II ended with the United States becoming the world's dominant power
   3. It remained to be seen how seriously the victorious Allies took their wartime rhetoric of freedom
      a. Atlantic Charter
      b. Mahatma Gandhi

## SUGGESTED DISCUSSION QUESTIONS

- Discuss the climate in America prior to the attack on Pearl Harbor. Was the general mood isolationist? Internationalist? Why?
- Evaluate FDR's Four Freedoms speech in *Voices of Freedom*.
- How did the United States pay for the war? What were the various economic tools used to raise money?
- Discuss the change in attitudes toward various ethnic groups during World War II such as Indians, Mexicans, and Asians. How were they treated? What freedoms were extended or contracted?
- Discuss the importance of the GI Bill of Rights to American society.
- What was the "double-V" campaign? How did the war spark a civil rights movement?

## SUPPLEMENTAL WEB AND VISUAL RESOURCES

U.S. Isolationism
*pbsvideodb.pbs.org/programs/chapter.asp?item_id=20877*
This site refers to the PBS film *The Finest Hour: The Battle of Britain,* which looks at the European war that raged while the United States continued with its policy of isolationism.

Blitzkrieg
*www.historylearningsite.co.uk/blitzkrieg.htm*
This site offers insight into many aspects of World War II as well as specific information on the German war tactic of blitzkrieg.

D-Day
*search.eb.com/normandy/*
This site contains information on the buildup for and the invasion of Normandy.

Life on the Home Front During World War II
*sandysq.gcinet.net/uss_salt_lake_city_ca25/homefrnt.htm*
This is a helpful site for a variety of perspectives of life in the United States during World War II.

Patriotic Art
*www.loc.gov/rr/print/swann/szyk/*
This Library of Congress site offers art and cartoons of World War II artist Arthur Szyk.

Japanese-American Internment
*www.oz.net/~cyu/internment/main.html*
This site is full of links to specific information pertaining to the internment of Japanese-Americans during World War II.

Zoot Suit Riots
*www.shop.pbs.org/*
This PBS "American Experience" video titled *The Zoot Suit Riots,* is a 60-minute film about the 1942 Latino riot in Los Angeles.

## SUPPLEMENTAL PRINT RESOURCES

Ambrose, Stephen. *Citizen Soldiers.* New York: Simon & Schuster, 1997.
Keegan, John. *The Battle For History: Re-Fighting World War II.* New York: Vintage, 1995.
Murray, Alice Yang. *What Did the Internment of Japanese Americans Mean?* New York: Bedford, 2000.
Newton, Wesley Phillips. *Montgomery in the Good War: Portrait of a Southern City, 1939–1946.* Tuscaloosa: University of Alabama Press, 2000.

Smith, Gaddis. *American Diplomacy During the Second World War, 1941–1945.* New Haven: Yale University Press, 1965.

Warren, Frank. *Noble Abstraction: American Liberal Intellectuals and World War II.* Columbus: Ohio State University Press, 1999.

Wingo, Josette Dermody. *Mother Was a Gunner's Mate: World War II in the Waves.* Annapolis: Naval Institute, 1994.

Winkler, Allan. *Home Front U.S.A.: America during World War II.* Wheeling, IL: Harlan Davidson, 2000.

## TEST BANK

### Matching

| | | | |
|---|---|---|---|
| e | 1. Wendell Willkie | a. | Spanish Civil War |
| f | 2. A. Philip Randolph | b. | *The American Century* |
| a | 3. Francisco Franco | c. | *An American Dilemma* |
| c | 4. Gunnar Myrdal | d. | ordered the use of the atomic bombs |
| h | 5. Winston Churchill | e. | *One World* |
| b | 6. Henry Luce | f. | Executive Order 8802 |
| i | 7. Joseph Stalin | g. | *The Road to Serfdom* |
| j | 8. Norman Rockwell | h. | Britain's prime minister |
| g | 9. Friedrich Hayek | i. | Soviet leader |
| d | 10. Harry Truman | j. | American painter |

| | | | |
|---|---|---|---|
| j | 1. "code talkers" | a. | interventionists |
| h | 2. Dumbarton Oaks | b. | appeasement |
| g | 3. Good Neighbor Policy | c. | "Big Three" meeting |
| a | 4. Freedom House | d. | blamed businessmen for World War I involvement |
| i | 5. Office of War Information | e. | Mexican agricultural workers |
| b | 6. Munich conference | f. | education for veterans |
| f | 7. GI Bill | g. | Latin America |
| c | 8. Yalta Conference | h. | United Nations |
| d | 9. Nye Committee | i. | mobilized American public opinion |
| e | 10. Bracero program | j. | Navajos |

### Multiple Choice

1. What was not one of the Four Freedoms expressed by FDR?
   a. freedom from want
   b. freedom of speech

    c. freedom from fear

  *d. freedom of enterprise

    e. freedom of religion

2. Who is considered the founder of fascism?

  *a. Benito Mussolini

    b. Adolf Hitler

    c. Francisco Franco

    d. Joseph Stalin

    e. Hideki Tojo

3. Many Americans were convinced by _____ that a policy of isolationism was necessary.

    a. the Atlantic Charter

  *b. Senator Gerald Nye's report

    c. FDR's Four Freedoms speech

    d. the Battle of Britain

    e. the attack on Pearl Harbor

4. Men like Henry Ford, Charles Lindbergh, and Father Francis Coughlin were members of the

    a. America Now! committee, an interventionist group

    b. Anti-Semitism Society, a group that blamed the Jews for the war

  *c. America First committee, an isolationist group

    d. Lend-Lease League, a group that supported technology for the war

    e. Free Paris Society, a group that advocated the liberation of Paris

5. Who was the only member of Congress to vote against a declaration of war on Japan after Pearl Harbor?

  *a. Jeanette Rankin

    b. Gerald Nye

    c. Wayne Morris

    d. Jane Addams

    e. Frances Perkins

6. During the war in Europe, Germany's advance into the Soviet Union was reversed at

    a. Moscow

    b. Kiev

    c. Leningrad

    d. Vladivostok

  *e. Stalingrad

7. Which area of the United States witnessed the greatest growth during the war?

    a. Northeast

    b. Midwest

   c. Southwest
*d. West Coast
   e. Southeast

8. The Office of War Information wished to
   a. give the war an ideological meaning
   b. mobilize public opinion
   c. utilize radio, film, and the press
   d. promote New Deal social programs
   *e. all of the above

9. Women working in defense industries during the war
   a. were viewed as permanent workers after the war, so long as they did a good job
   *b. were told by advertisers that they were fighting for freedom
   c. did not make much difference in the war effort
   d. were small in number, as most women took clerical work or joined the military service as nurses
   e. were all young, single women who left their jobs once they got married

10. What did Henry Luce and Henry Wallace have in common?
    a. They both believed that the United States should assume an isolationist policy, leading by example, not by action
    b. They were both liberals in their political beliefs and strongly supported the New Deal, which they believed should be spread to the rest of the world
    *c. They both put forth a new conception of America's role in the world based in part on internationalism and the idea that the American experience should serve as a model for all other nations
    d. They both believed that the best course of action for the United States after the war was conservative fiscal policies, including high tariffs and domestic taxes
    e. They were both working for the Office of War Information in promoting, through books, the positions held by the group America First

11. Which work offered an intellectual justification for opponents of active government, laying the foundation for the rise of modern conservatism?
    a. Henry Luce's *American Century*
    *b. Friedrich Hayek's *The Road to Serfdom*
    c. Wendell Willkie's *One World*
    d. Gunnar Myrdal's *An American Dilemma*
    e. Ruth Benedict's *Races and Racism*

12. Which statement about the Japanese-American internment is false?
    a. The press supported the policy of internment almost unanimously
    b. The Supreme Court refused to intervene

      c. Japanese-Americans in Hawaii were exempt from the policy

      d. Japan used it as proof that America was racist toward non-white peoples

   *e. Once the FBI did background checks on individuals they were free to leave the camps and return home

13. A. Philip Randolph
      a. was instrumental in getting the GI Bill of Rights passed
      b. fought for the release of the Japanese-Americans
   *c. pressured FDR to issue Executive Order 8802
      d. was the first black captain in the U.S. Army
      e. led a group of workers in the CIO in a strike against U.S. Steel

14. What was the "double-V" campaign?
   *a. an attempt to gain victory in Germany and an end to segregation in America
      b. an effort by the government to encourage Americans to conserve resources
      c. America's military campaign indicating victory in Germany and Japan
      d. a British propaganda campaign before Pearl Harbor trying to get the United States to enter the war
      e. FDR's slogan for winning the war on the front lines and through production on the home front

15. According to Gunnar Myrdal, what was America's dilemma?
      a. a conflict between its rhetoric at home and its foreign policy abroad
   *b. a conflict between American values and American racial policies
      c. a conflict between American business ethos and American labor unions
      d. a conflict between America's isolationism and Germany's aggression
      e. a conflict between American liberalism and American conservatism

16. Approximately _____ persons died immediately after the atomic bomb was dropped on Hiroshima.
      a. 30,000
      b. 50,000
   *c. 70,000
      d. 90,000
      e. 110,000

17. At Yalta the "Big Three" met for a summit. What was finally agreed to at this meeting?
   *a. the Soviet Union would enter the Pacific war
      b. plans for a United Nations
      c. the use of atomic weapons to end the war
      d. Churchill would give up the British colonial possessions
      e. placing top Nazi leaders on trial for war crimes

18. The World Bank and International Monetary Fund were established at
    a. Dumbarton Oaks
    b. Tehran
    c. Bermuda
    *d. Bretton Woods
    e. Potsdam

19. Which statement about the Atlantic Charter is true?
    a. It was made between Stalin and Hitler
    b. It outlawed submarine warfare
    *c. It endorsed the freedoms from want and fear
    d. It established the World Bank and GATT
    e. It established the United Nations

## True or False

T    1. To Roosevelt, the Four Freedoms expressed deeply held American values worthy of being spread worldwide.

F    2. The Good Neighbor Policy was extended primarily toward Canada to lend support in her efforts to aid Britain against German aggression.

T    3. Until 1941, 80 percent of Japan's oil supply came from the United States.

F    4. When war broke out in Europe in 1939, the Soviet Union stood virtually alone in fighting Germany.

F    5. The Freedom House was a place of refuge for Jews who had escaped the Holocaust.

T    6. The largest surrender in American military history occurred at the Philippines, after the Japanese took over the island.

F    7. Only Jewish people were killed during the German Holocaust.

F    8. After opening up a second front following the success of the Normandy invasion on D-Day, British and American troops inflicted devastating damage upon the Germans, resulting in over 80 percent of German causalities.

T    9. Organized labor entered a three-sided arrangement with government and business that allowed union membership to soar to unprecedented levels.

F    10. Women working in defense industry jobs made great strides in achieving equal rights, culminating in the passage of the Nineteenth Amendment, which granted women's suffrage.

T    11. Henry Luce, author of *The American Century,* saw a leadership role for the United States in the postwar world.

T    12. Since the enemy (Germany and Japan) used racism, racism and nativism had been stripped of intellectual respectability in America, particularly with the publication of Ruth Benedict's *Race and Racism.*

F    13. The "zoot suit" riots were between the police of Detroit and the black workers of the city.

T    14. The war experience brought many more American Indians closer to the mainstream of American life.

T    15. Japanese propaganda depicted Americans as a self-indulgent people contaminated by ethnic and racial diversity as opposed to the racially "pure" Japanese.

F    16. The majority of the Japanese-Americans that were interned during the war were not actually citizens of the United States.

F    17. During the war, the AFL made great strides in helping blacks and was more racially integrated than any union had ever been before.

T    18. By 1945, support for racial justice had finally taken its place on the liberal-left agenda alongside full employment, civil liberties, and the expansion of the New Deal welfare state.

T    19. The dropping of the atomic bomb was the logical culmination of the way World War II had been fought.

T    20. The Bretton Woods meeting established a new international economic system.

## Short Answer

*Identify and give the historical significance of each of the following terms, events, and people in a paragraph or two.*

1. "zoot suit" riots
2. double-V campaign
3. Lend-Lease
4. atomic bomb
5. Executive Order 8802
6. Japanese Internment
7. Bretton Woods conference
8. Four Freedoms
9. The Fifth Freedom
10. liberalism

## Essay Questions

1. Describe how government military spending during the war affected the economic development of the West and South.

2. World War II redrew the boundaries of American nationality. Defend this statement by comparing the experiences of first-generation immigrants, second-generation immigrants, and blacks during World War I with their experiences during World War II.

3. Explain the relationship between labor and the government during the war. Be sure to discuss strikes, company owners, federal legislation, and minorities in your essay. Did the war help the labor movement? Why or why not?

4. What significance was there in the *Saturday Evening Post*'s assigning Filipino poet Carlos Bulosan to write the essay that accompanied Norman Rockwell's illustration for the Freedom from Want?

5. Explain how the reports of the National Resources Planning Board reflected the shift, seen in the late 1930s, in liberals' outlook toward the government and the economy.

6. Analyze how the rhetoric of World War II brought the contradiction between the principle of equal freedom and the actual status of blacks to the forefront of national life.

7. Thinking back to previous chapters, analyze the validity of Franklin Roosevelt's statement that to be an American had always been a "matter of mind and heart" and "never . . . a matter of race or ancestry." Your answer should include a discussion about blacks and different immigrants, including Asians, Irish, and "new immigrants."

8. One black woman said about the war that it was Hitler that got blacks out of the white folks' kitchen. Explain what the war did for blacks. How did they "move out of the kitchen" and what forces were behind those achievements?

9. World War II is often referred to as "The Good War." Evaluate that title for the war. Is it appropriate? Why, or why not?

**CHAPTER 23**

# The United States and the Cold War, 1945–1953

This chapter concentrates on the history of the early Cold War period and the Truman administration. The chapter opens with the national tour of the Freedom Train, which celebrated the freedom of America in contrast to the tyranny of Hitler. The chapter continues by explaining the origins of the Cold War, the roots of containment as outlined by George Kennan and implemented through the Truman Doctrine, Marshall Plan, Berlin Airlift, and Korean War. Many critics, including Walter Lippmann, questioned the wisdom of viewing the Cold War through the narrow lens of "free versus slave." Next, freedom and the Cold War are explored by comparing freedom with totalitarianism. The quest for an international human rights movement begins with the United Nation's Universal Declaration of Human Rights, a document that the United States has still not completely ratified. Truman's domestic policy, the Fair Deal, is an attempt to continue the expansion of government under the New Deal. Truman wished to extend rights to labor and blacks, as well as create a comprehensive national health insurance and housing plans. Most of Truman's agenda was stopped by the Republican resurgence led by Senator Taft. The Democratic Party was disrupted with the Dixiecrat revolt and Henry Wallace's Progressive Party, but Truman was still able to steal the 1948 election away from the Republican Thomas Dewey. The chapter concludes with the anticommunist crusade, looking at the HUAC investigations, the arrest of the Rosenbergs, and the rise of Senator Joseph McCarthy. The loyalty of every American came under suspicion during the Red Scare. As such, critics such as historian Henry Steele Commager spoke out against the blatant violations of the First Amendment. His article "Who is Loyal to America?" is highlighted in *Voices of Freedom*.

## CHAPTER OUTLINE

A. The Two Powers
   1. The United States emerged from World War II as by far the world's greatest power
   2. The only power that in any way could rival the United States was the Soviet Union
B. The Roots of Containment
   1. It seems all but inevitable that the two major powers to emerge from the war would come into conflict
   2. Many Americans became convinced that Stalin was violating the promise of free election in Poland agreed to at the Yalta conference of 1945
   3. The Long Telegram advised the Truman administration that the Soviets could not be dealt with as a normal government
      a. "Containment"
      b. Iron Curtain speech
C. The Truman Doctrine
   1. Truman soon determined to put the policy of containment into effect
   2. To rally popular backing for Greece and Turkey, Truman rolled out the heaviest weapon in his rhetorical arsenal—the defense of freedom
   3. The Truman Doctrine created the language through which most Americans came to understand the postwar world
   4. Truman's rhetoric suggested that the United States had assumed a permanent global responsibility
D. The Marshall Plan
   1. George Marshall pledged the United States to contribute billions of dollars to finance the economic recovery of Europe
   2. The Marshall Plan offered a positive vision to go along with containment
      a. The Marshall Plan envisioned a New Deal for Europe
   3. The Marshall Plan proved to be one of the most successful foreign aid programs in history
E. The Berlin Blockade and NATO
   1. In 1945 the Soviets cut off road and rail traffic from the American, British, and French zones of occupied Germany to Berlin
      a. An eleven-month allied airlift followed
   2. In 1949 the Soviet Union tested its first atomic bomb
   3. The North Atlantic Treaty Organization (NATO) pledged mutual defense against any future Soviet attack
      a. Warsaw Pact
   4. Communists won the civil war in China in 1949
   5. In the wake of these events, the National Security Council approved a call for a permanent military buildup to enable the United States to pursue a global crusade against communism
      a. NSC 68

    F. The Korean War
       1. In June 1950, the North Korean army invaded the South, hoping to
         · reunify the country under Communist control
       2. American troops did the bulk of the fighting on this first battlefield of
         the Cold War
         a. General Douglas MacArthur
       3. Korea made it clear that the Cold War, which began in Europe, had
         become a global conflict
       4. Taken together, the events of 1947–53 showed that the world had been
         divided in two
    G. Cold War Critics
       1. Casting the Cold War in terms of a worldwide battle between freedom
         and slavery had unfortunate consequences
       2. Walter Lippmann objected to turning foreign policy into an
         "ideological crusade"
    H. The Free World
       1. Although America granted independence to the Philippines in 1946,
         much of Europe intended to keep their empire
       2. Economics and geopolitical interests motivated American
         foreign policy, but the language of freedom was used to justify its
         actions

III. The Cold War and the Idea of Freedom
    A. The Cultural Cold War
       1. One of the more unusual Cold War battlefields involved American
         history and culture
         a. Hollywood
       2. The Central Intelligence Agency and Defense Department emerged as
         unlikely patrons of the arts
    B. Freedom and Totalitarianism
       1. Works produced by artists who considered themselves thoroughly
         nonpolitical became weapons in the cultural Cold War
         a. Jackson Pollock
         b. The New York School
       2. Along with freedom, the Cold War's other great mobilizing concept
         was "totalitarianism"
       3. Totalitarianism left no room for individual rights or alternative values
         and therefore could never change from within
         a. McCarran Internal Security Act
       4. Just as the conflict over slavery redefined American freedom in the
         nineteenth century, and the confrontation with the Nazis shaped
         understandings of freedom during World War II, the Cold War
         reshaped them once again

C. The Rise of Human Rights
   1. The idea that rights exist applicable to all members of the human family originated during the eighteenth century in the Enlightenment and the American and French Revolutions
   2. In 1948, the United Nations General Assembly approved the Universal Declaration of Human Rights
   3. After the Cold War ended, the idea of human rights would play an increasingly prominent role in world affairs
      a. Freedom House

IV. The Truman Presidency
   A. The Fair Deal
      1. Truman's first domestic task was to preside over the transition from a wartime to a peacetime economy
      2. Truman moved to revive the stalled momentum of the New Deal
   B. The Postwar Strike Wave
      1. The AFL and CIO launched Operation Dixie, a campaign to bring unionization to the South
      2. In 1946, nearly 5 million workers went on strike
      3. President Truman feared the strikes would seriously disrupt the economy
   C. The Republican Resurgence
      1. Republicans swept to control both houses of Congress in 1946
      2. Congress turned aside Truman's Fair Deal program
         a. Taft-Harley Act
   D. Postwar Civil Rights
      1. Immediately after the war, the status of black Americans enjoyed a prominence in national affairs unmatched since Reconstruction
      2. The Brooklyn Dodgers added Jackie Robinson to their team in 1947
   E. To Secure These Rights
      1. A Commission on Civil Rights appointed by the president issued *To Secure These Rights*
         a. It called on the federal government to abolish segregation and discrimination
      2. In 1948, Truman presented an ambitious civil rights program to Congress
         a. Truman desegregated the armed forces
      3. The Democratic platform of 1948 was the most progressive in the party's history
   F. The Dixiecrat and Wallace Revolts
      1. Dixiecrats formed the States' Rights Party
         a. Strom Thurmond

      2. A group of left-wing critics of Truman's foreign policy formed the Progressive Party

         a. Henry Wallace

   G. The 1948 Campaign

      1. Truman's main opponent was the colorless Republican Thomas A. Dewey

      2. Truman's success represented one of the greatest upsets in American political history

V. The Anticommunist Crusade

      1. The Cold War encouraged a culture of secrecy and dishonesty

      2. At precisely the moment when the United States celebrated freedom as the foundation of American life, the right to dissent came under attack

   A. Loyalty and Disloyalty

      1. Those who could be linked to communism were enemies of freedom

      2. HUAC hearings against Hollywood began in 1947

   B. The Spy Trials

      1. HUAC investigation against Alger Hiss

      2. The Rosenbergs were convicted for spying and executed in 1953

   C. McCarthy and McCarthyism

      1. Senator Joseph McCarthy announced in 1950 that he had a list of 205 Communists working for the State Department

      2. McCarthy's downfall came with nationally televised Army-McCarthy hearings in 1954

   D. An Atmosphere of Fear

      1. Anticommunism was as much a local as a national phenomenon

         a. "Red squads"

         b. Private organizations

      2. Local anticommunist groups forced public libraries to remove "un-American" books from their shelves

      3. The courts did nothing to halt the political repression

         a. *Dennis v. United States*

   E. The Uses of Anticommunism

      1. Anticommunism had many faces and purposes

      2. Anticommunism also served as a weapon wielded by individuals and groups in battles unrelated to defending the United States against subversion

      3. The anticommunist crusade promoted a new definition of loyalty—conformity

         a. Henry Steele Commager

   F. Anticommunist Politics

      1. The McCarran Internal Security Bill of 1950

      2. The McCarran-Walter Act of 1952

G. Cold War Civil Rights
1. Every political and social organization had to cooperate with the anticommunist crusade or face destruction
   a. Organized labor rid itself of its left-wing officials and emerged as a major supporter of the foreign policy of the Cold War
2. The civil rights movement also underwent a transformation
   a. The NAACP purged Communists from local branches
3. The Cold War caused a shift in thinking and tactics among civil rights groups
4. Dean Acheson's speech to the Delta Council was filled with irony
5. After 1948, little came of the Truman administration's civil rights flurry, but time would reveal that the waning of the civil rights impulse was only temporary

## SUGGESTED DISCUSSION QUESTIONS

- Discuss what George Kennan outlined in his Long Telegram and explain how it was put into effect.
- How was the language of freedom used to justify American foreign policy in the early Cold War? What were the consequences of viewing the Cold War in such narrow terms of "free versus slave"?
- What was the core principle of the UN's Universal Declaration of Human Rights?
- Describe Truman's Fair Deal. How successful was it, and why?
- How was labor affected during the Red Scare?
- Debate the Red Scare in terms of national security versus freedoms protected by the First Amendment. Do you agree or disagree with the *Voices of Freedom* excerpt?

## SUPPLEMENTAL WEB AND VISUAL RESOURCES

Cold War Beginnings
*www.historyteacher.net/APUSH-Course/ Weblinks/ Weblinks25.htm*
This site covers the first decade of the Cold War. It has an extensive list of Web links and primary source documents.

The Marshall Plan
*www.marshallfoundation.org/ about_gcm/ marshall_plan.htm*
This site covers the summary, origin, and text of the Marshall Plan, with useful pictures to accompany it.

Korean War

*korea50.army.mil/ history/ index.shtml*
This helpful site has a historical perspective on the Korean War with
chronologies, maps, and bibliographies.

President Harry Truman

*www.trumanlibrary.org/ library.htm*
This site is produced by the Truman Presidential Museum and contains a
wealth of material on Truman's presidency.

Harry Truman

*www.pbs.org/ wgbh/ amex/ truman/*
From the PBS "American Experience" series, Truman is documented with a
timeline and picture galleries.

## SUPPLEMENTAL PRINT RESOURCES

Beisner, Robert. "The Secretary, the Spy, and the Sage: Dean Acheson, Alger
Hiss, and George Kennan." *Diplomatic History*, 27, no. 1 (2003): 1–14.
Frederickson, Kari. *The Dixiecrat Revolt and the End of the Solid South,
1932–1968*. Chapel Hill: University of North Carolina Press, 2001.
Fried, Albert. *McCarthyism: The Great American Red Scare: A Documentary
History*. New York: Oxford University Press, 1997.
Gaddis, John Lewis. *We Now Know: Rethinking Cold War History*. New York:
Oxford University Press, 1997.
Gardner, Michael. *Harry Truman and Civil Rights: Moral Courage and Political
Risks*. Carbondale: Southern Illinois University Press, 2002.
Hixon, Walter. *George Kennan: Cold War Iconoclast*. New York: Columbia
University Press, 1989.
de Luna, Phyllis Komarek. *Public Versus Private Power During the Truman
Administration: A Study of Fair Deal Liberalism*. New York: Peter Lang, 1997.
White, John Kenneth. *Still Seeing Red: How the Cold War Shapes the New
American Politics*. Boulder: Westview Press, 1997.

## TEST BANK

### Matching

| | | | |
|---|---|---|---|
| e | 1. Alger Hiss | a. | alleged nuclear spies |
| d | 2. Walter Lippmann | b. | Korean War commander |
| j | 3. Joe McCarthy | c. | 1948 Progressive Party candidate |
| b | 4. Douglas MacArthur | d. | critic of the Cold War |

| | | | |
|---|---|---|---|
| g | 5. George Kennan | e. | prosecuted by HUAC |
| i | 6. Harry Truman | f. | "Who is Loyal to America?" |
| h | 7. Jackie Robinson | g. | author of "containment" doctrine |
| c | 8. Henry Wallace | h. | black baseball star |
| a | 9. Rosenbergs | i. | Fair Deal |
| f | 10. Henry Steele Commager | j. | Senator from Wisconsin |

| | | | |
|---|---|---|---|
| d | 1. States' Rights Party | a. | unionization to the South |
| g | 2. Freedom Train | b. | set quotas on immigrants |
| i | 3. Fair Deal | c. | Greece and Turkey |
| j | 4. Marshall Plan | d. | Dixiecrats |
| f | 5. Taft-Hartley Act | e. | outlined containment policy |
| h | 6. NATO | f. | slave labor bill |
| c | 7. Truman Doctrine | g. | a traveling exhibition |
| a | 8. Operation Dixie | h. | first peacetime alliance for the United States |
| e | 9. Long Telegram | i. | Truman's domestic program |
| b | 10. McCarran-Walter Act | j. | economic aid to Europe |

## Multiple Choice

1. The Freedom Train
   *a. was a traveling exhibition of over 100 historical documents
   b. was the first desegregated passenger train in the South
   c. was what union sympathizers referred to during the Pullman Strike
   d. was the name given to the caravan of airplanes that brought supplies to Berlin
   e. was what Harry Truman called his 1948 election campaign

2. One of the reasons that the Soviet Union felt justified in making demands upon the Western world was because of the enormous sacrifice it made to World War II, which is estimated at _____ million dead.
   a. 2
   b. 8
   c. 15
   *d. 20
   e. 30

3. George Kennan's Long Telegram outlined the containment policy. What actually put the policy into effect?
   a. Truman Doctrine
   b. Marshall Plan
   c. Berlin Airlift

    d. Korean War

  *e. all of the above

4. What program was in effect to bring a New Deal for Europe?
    a. the Fair Deal
    b. Operation European Freedom
  *c. the Marshall Plan
    d. the North Atlantic Treaty Organization (NATO)
    e. the Truman Doctrine

5. How did the United States respond to Joseph Stalin's blockade around Berlin?
  *a. Truman ordered that supplies be brought to Berlin via an airlift
    b. Truman put American forces on high alert and threatened atomic war if Stalin did not lift the blockade
    c. Truman ignored it
    d. Truman asked the United Nations to place an embargo on all goods going to the Soviet Union
    e. American forces forced their way through the road blockade with a caravan of armored tanks

6. Which idea best describes what NSC-68 called for?
    a. patience on the part of the United States in dealing with the Soviet Union
  *b. a permanent military buildup and a global application of containment
    c. limited strategic goals, confronting the Soviets only at key industrial areas
    d. a sole reliance on nuclear weapons while demobilizing conventional forces
    e. all of the above

7. Which statement about the Korean conflict is false?
    a. The United Nations authorized the use of forces to repel the North Koreans
  *b. Chinese troops threatened to enter the conflict, but never did
    c. General MacArthur argued for an invasion of China and for the use of nuclear weapons
    d. Truman removed General MacArthur from his command when he publicly criticized Truman
    e. The war ended in a cease fire, not with a formal peace treaty

8. Who led the New York School of painters?
    a. Norman Rockwell
    b. Pablo Picasso
  *c. Jackson Pollock
    d. Walter Lippmann
    e. Arthur Szyk

9. In 1948, Eleanor Roosevelt chaired a committee to draft what?
    a. the GI Bill of Rights
    b. the Economic Bill of Rights
    c. the Declaration of the Rights of Man
    *d. the Universal Declaration of Human Rights
    e. the Civil Rights Act

10. All of the following were goals of the Fair Deal except
    a. expanding public housing
    *b. passing the Taft-Hartley Act
    c. increasing the minimum wage
    d. creating a national health insurance program
    e. expanding Social Security coverage

11. Which civil rights measure was passed into law during Truman's administration?
    a. federal law against lynching
    *b. desegregation of the armed forces
    c. establishment of a permanent federal civil rights commission
    d. federal law against poll taxes
    e. protection for equal access to jobs and education

12. What piece of American legislation stated that union leaders had to swear an oath that they were not Communists?
    a. House Un-American Activities Committee Act
    b. Truman Federal Employee Loyalty Act
    *c. Taft-Hartley Act
    d. CIO-AFL Act
    e. Smith Act

13. Who did the States' Rights Party nominate for president in 1948?
    *a. Strom Thurmond
    b. Henry Wallace
    c. Joe McCarthy
    d. George Wallace
    e. Thomas Dewey

14. What reason did the "Hollywood Ten" give for not cooperating with the HUAC hearings?
    a. They were all Communists and did not want to indict themselves
    b. Ronald Reagan had threatened that they would lose their jobs if they cooperated
    c. They were all busy making movies and did not have time to attend the hearings
    *d. They felt the hearings were a violation of the First Amendment

e. As Republicans, they were insulted that their loyalty was being
questioned

15. Who did Whittaker Chambers accuse of being a Soviet spy during a HUAC
hearing?
    a. Julius Rosenberg
    b. Richard Nixon
    *c. Alger Hiss
    d. David Greenglass
    e. Robert Oppenheimer

16. Joe McCarthy announced that he had a list of 205 Communists who worked
for
    *a. the State Department
    b. the Department of the Interior
    c. the Federal Bureau of Investigation
    d. the Labor Department
    e. the White House

17. Who were the common victims of McCarthyism?
    a. known Communists
    b. immigrants from Russia and Germany
    *c. virtually anyone who refused to cooperate with the investigations
    d. teachers and university professors
    e. military servicemen

18. *Dennis v. United States*
    a. made it illegal to jail Communists
    b. allowed the deportation of suspected Communists
    c. forbade the Communist Party from existing in the United States
    *d. upheld the jailing of Communists
    e. allowed universities to fire professors who taught the theories of Marx

19. In "Who is Loyal to America?" Henry Steele Commager
    a. supports the efforts of people like Senator McCarthy
    b. favors the new meaning given to loyalty of conformity
    c. believes that the Communists in America pose a serious threat
    d. is bitter since he was accused of having communist sympathies by HUAC
    *e. believes that the narrow definition of loyalty denies freedom of thought

20. Organized labor emerged
    a. as a vocal critic of McCarthyism
    *b. as a major supporter of the foreign policy of the Cold War
    c. as a radical wing of the Communist Party
    d. as a militant group willing to fight the Red Scare
    e. as the best informants for the FBI and HUAC

## True or False

F    1. The Freedom Train contained documents such as the Wagner Act and FDR's Four Freedoms speech.

T    2. George Kennan's Long Telegram laid the foundation for the policy of containment.

F    3. Harry Truman always expected to be president some day.

F    4. The Truman Doctrine supported giving billions of dollars for European economic recovery.

F    5. Overall, despite good intentions, the Marshall Plan was not very successful.

T    6. The North Atlantic Treaty was the first long-term military alliance between the United States and Europe since the Treaty of Amity and Commerce with France during the American Revolution.

T    7. The Berlin Airlift made it clear that Truman was determined to deny the Soviet Union any victories in the Cold War.

T    8. The Korean War became the first American conflict fought by an integrated army since the War for Independence.

T    9. Generally speaking, economics and geopolitical interests motivated American foreign policy, but the language of freedom was used to justify its actions.

F    10. Hollywood remained the one voice of protest during the Red Scare, making films that celebrated individualism, socialism, and the questioning of authority.

T    11. Totalitarianism had become a shorthand way of describing those on the other side in the Cold War.

F    12. The United States was the first country to approve both covenants of the UN's Universal Declaration of Human Rights.

F    13. In an attempt to shatter the hold of anti-labor conservatives in the South, the AFL and the CIO launched Operation Reconstruction.

T    14. In 1952, for the first time since record keeping began seventy years earlier, no lynchings took place in the United States.

F    15. The Democratic platform in 1948 was fairly conservative, showing that Truman knew his reelection would be close.

T    16. Harry Truman's reelection in 1948 was one of the greatest upsets in American political history.

T    17. Joe McCarthy's downfall came with the nationally televised Army-McCarthy hearings in 1954.

T    18. Both the Taft-Hartley Act and the McCarran-Walter Act passed over Truman's veto.

T    19. The CIO, which had a long history of communist members, purged over 1 million workers from its ranks during the Red Scare.

F    20. Considering there were very few radicals involved in the civil rights movement, groups like the NAACP were completely unaffected by the Red Scare.

## Short Answer

*Identify and give the historical significance of each of the following terms, events, and people in a paragraph or two.*

1. Truman Doctrine
2. Marshall Plan
3. Korean War
4. HUAC
5. Freedom Train
6. Fair Deal
7. Joseph McCarthy
8. Henry Wallace
9. Taft-Hartley Act
10. loyalty

## Essay Questions

1. Analyze the policy of containment. Was the United States correct to think of the Soviet Union as expansionist and as a threat to American liberty?

2. Describe how the Cold War was fought abroad. Be sure to discuss how freedom was used in justifying U.S. actions.

3. Comment upon Henry Luce's statement that "freedom" was the best word he could use to explain America to the rest of the world. Why do you think he picked that word? How did the Cold War affect his choice? Do you think that Luce was correct, or would you pick a different word to describe America to the rest of the world in 1952?

4. The Cold War impacted every aspect of American life. Discuss the domestic implications of the Cold War. Your essay should explain how the Cold War affected higher education, the economy, immigration policy, civil rights, and civil liberties.

5. By 1952 the Cold War was cast in terms of a worldwide battle between freedom and slavery. Explain (1) how the Cold War had come to be seen that way, (2) events that illustrate that view, and (3) the historical consequences of such a view.

6. Evaluate Harry Truman's domestic policy. What parts of it reflected the New Deal? Why was it so difficult to implement? How did it expand freedom for Americans? How did it restrict freedom?

7. Describe how the Cold War helped to reshape freedom's meaning, identifying it ever more closely with anticommunism, "free enterprise," and the defense of the social and economic status quo. You may wish to include information from the *Voices of Freedom* excerpt in your answer.

8. Fully discuss and examine the limitations placed upon freedom during the Cold War. Then compare those circumstances with those during the Red Scare after World War I. What was the same? What was different? Were restrictions on civil liberties justified in both cases? Why, or why not? How did Americans react in each era?

| An Affluent Society, 1953–1960

This chapter concentrates on the history of the 1950s and its economic prosperity, its conformity and cultural critics, and the civil rights movement. Opening with the Richard Nixon and Nikita Khrushchev debates in 1959, the chapter sets up the theme of the suburban material bliss of the 1950s. The "golden age" of the 1950s is discussed, identifying a new meaning of freedom for the American people in consumerism and the freedom of consumer choice. The Cold War fueled industrial production and promoted a redistribution of the nation's population and economic resources. Likewise, the Cold War also shaped a new role for women and the family. Left out of this economic prosperity and growing suburbia were blacks and ethnic minorities, who found themselves left in the inner cities. The chapter then examines the Eisenhower administration. Calling his policies modern Republicanism, Eisenhower did not roll back the New Deal, but instead extended the core New Deal programs. Labor too benefited from the prosperity of the decade. In foreign policy, Eisenhower adopted the policy of "massive retaliation" to fight the Cold War and used the CIA in various Third World countries to counter nationalist movements which were viewed as Soviet-sponsored communist campaigns. Responding to the affluence and the anxieties of the Cold War, cultural critics of the 1950s spoke out against the conformity they witnessed. From sociologist David Riesman to the poems of the Beats, cultural critics voiced dissent. The final section of the chapter discusses the civil rights movement. Building upon decades, the movement gets its momentum from the *Brown v. Board of Education* decision, the Montgomery Bus Boycott, and the leadership of Martin Luther King, Jr. Mobilizing the black community in Montgomery, King's oratory abilities and his definition of freedom are highlighted in *Voices of Freedom*. The chapter concludes with the 1960 election between Nixon and John F. Kennedy.

I. The Nixon-Khrushchev "kitchen-debates"

II. The Golden Age
   A. The Golden Age

   1. After the war, the American economy enjoyed remarkable growth
   2. Numerous innovations came into widespread use during these years, transforming Americans' daily lives
B. A Changing Economy
   1. The Cold War fueled industrial production and promoted a redistribution of the nation's population and economic resources
   2. Since the 1950s, the American economy has shifted away from manufacturing
   3. The number of farms had declined since the 1950s, but production increased
      a. The center of gravity of American farming shifted decisively to Texas, Arizona, and especially California
C. The Growth of Suburbia
   1. The main engines of economic growth during the 1950s were residential construction and spending on consumer goods
   2. The dream of home ownership came within reach of the majority of Americans
      a. Levittown
   3. California became the most prominent symbol of the postwar suburban boom
   4. Western cities were decentralized clusters of single-family homes and businesses united by a web of highways
D. A Consumer Culture
   1. In a consumer culture, the measure of freedom became the ability to gratify market desires
   2. Americans became comfortable living in never-ending debt, once seen as a loss of economic freedom
   3. Consumer culture demonstrated the superiority of the American way of life to communism
E. The TV World
   1. Television replaced newspapers as the most common source of information about public events and provided Americans of all regions and backgrounds with a common cultural experience
   2. TV avoided controversy and projected a bland image of middle-class life
   3. Television also became the most effective advertising medium ever invented
F. A New Ford
   1. Along with a home and television set, the car became part of what sociologists called "the standard consumer package" of the 1950s
   2. Auto manufacturers and oil companies vaulted to the top ranks of corporate America
   3. The automobile transformed the nation's daily life

G. The Female Sphere
1. After 1945, women lost most of the industrial jobs they had performed during the war
2. By the mid-1950s women were working again, but the nature and aims of women's work had changed
3. Women were expected to get married, have children, and stay at home
   a. Baby boom
H. The Cold War Family
1. The family also became a weapon in the Cold War
   a. Feminism seemed to have disappeared from American life
I. A Segregated Landscape
1. The suburbs remained segregated communities
J. Building Segregation
1. During the postwar suburban boom, federal agencies continued to insure mortgages that barred resale of houses to non-whites, thereby financing housing segregation
2. A Housing Act passed by Congress in 1949 authorized the construction of over 800,000 units of public housing in order to provide a "decent home for every American family"
3. Suburbanization hardened the racial lines of division in American life
   a. Seven million whites left the cities for the suburbs while three million blacks moved into cities
   b. Puerto Ricans
K. The Divided Society
1. The process of racial exclusion became self-reinforcing
   a. Whites viewed urban ghettos as places of crime, poverty, and welfare
   b. "Blockbusting"
2. Suburban home ownership long remained a white entitlement
L. The End of Ideology
1. To many observers in the 1950s it seemed that the ills of American society had been solved
   a. If problems remained, their solution required technical adjustments, not structural chance or aggressive political intervention
M. Protestant-Catholic-Jew
1. There emerged a new "Judeo-Christian" heritage, a notion that became central to the cultural and political dialogue of the 1950s
2. The idea of a unified Judeo-Christian tradition reflected the decline of anti-Semitism and anti-Catholicism in the wake of World War II
   a. Secularization
N. Selling Free Enterprise
1. More than political democracy or freedom of speech, an economic system resting on private ownership united the nations of the Free World

2. The "selling of free enterprise" became a major industry
  a. The Advertising Council
O. "People's Capitalism"
  1. Until well into the twentieth century, most ordinary Americans had been deeply suspicious of big business
  2. Large-scale production was not only necessary to fighting the Cold War, it enhanced freedom by multiplying consumer goods
    a. Stock market

III. The Eisenhower Era
  A. Ike and Nixon
    1. General Dwight Eisenhower ran for president in 1952
    2. Richard Nixon ran as his vice president
      a. Nixon gained a reputation for opportunism and dishonesty
  B. The 1952 Campaign
    1. Nixon's "Checkers speech" rescued his political career
      a. It illustrated the importance of TV in politics
    2. Eisenhower's popularity and promises to end the Korean conflict brought him victory in 1952
    3. During the 1950s, voters at home and abroad seemed to find reassurance in selecting familiar, elderly leaders to govern them
  C. Modern Republicanism
    1. Wealthy businessmen dominated Eisenhower's cabinet
      a. Eisenhower refused to roll back the New Deal
    2. Modern Republicanism aimed to sever the Republican Party's identification in the minds of many Americans with Herbert Hoover, the Great Depression, and indifference to the economic conditions of ordinary citizens
      a. Core New Deal programs expanded
    3. Government spending was used to promote productivity and boost employment
      a. Interstate Highway Act
      b. National Defense Education Act
  D. The Social Contract
    1. The 1950s witnessed an easing of the labor conflict of the two previous decades
      a. AFL and CIO merged in 1955
      b. Social contract
    2. Unionized workers shared fully in 1950s prosperity
  E. Massive Retaliation
    1. Ike took office at a time when the Cold War had entered an extremely dangerous phase
    2. "Massive retaliation" declared that any Soviet attack on an American ally would be countered by a nuclear assault on the Soviet Union itself
    3. Critics called the doctrine "brinksmanship"

    F. Ike and the Russians

        1. Eisenhower came to believe that the Soviets were reasonable and could be dealt with in conventional diplomatic terms

        2. Khrushchev's call for "peaceful coexistence" with the United States raised the possibility of an easing of the Cold War

        3. In 1958, the two superpowers agreed to voluntarily halt the testing of nuclear weapons

    G. The Emergence of the Third World

        1. The post–World War II era witnessed the crumbling of European empires

        2. Decolonization presented the United States with a complex set of choices

    H. The Cold War in the Third World

        1. The Cold War became the determining factor in American relations with the Third World

           a. Guatemala

           b. Iran

        2. The Suez Crisis in 1956 led to the "Eisenhower Doctrine"

    I. Origins of the Vietnam War

        1. Anticommunism led the United States into deeper and deeper involvement in Vietnam

        2. A peace conference in Geneva divided Vietnam temporarily at the seventeenth parallel

        3. Events in Guatemala, Iran, and Vietnam, considered great successes at the time by American policymakers, cast a long shadow over American foreign relations

    J. Mass Society and Its Critics

        1. Some intellectuals wondered whether the celebration of affluence and the either-or mentality of the Cold War obscured the extent to which the United States itself fell short of the ideal of freedom

           a. Hans J. Morgenthau

           b. C. Wright Mills

        2. One strand of social analysis in the 1950s contended that Americans did not enjoy genuine freedom

           a. David Riesman's *The Lonely Crowd*

        3. Some commentators feared that the Russians had demonstrated a greater ability to sacrifice for common public goals than Americans

           a. John Kenneth Galbraith's *The Affluent Society*

           b. William Whyte's *The Organization Man*

    K. Rebels Without a Cause

        1. The emergence of a popular culture geared to the emerging youth market suggested that significant generational tensions lay beneath the bland surface of 1950s life

    2. Cultural life during the 1950s seemed far more daring than politics
      a. Rock and roll
      b. *Playboy*
  L. The Beats
    1. The Beats were a small group of poets and writers who railed against mainstream culture
    2. Rejecting the work ethic, the "desperate materialism" of the suburban middle class, and the militarization of American life by the Cold War, the Beats celebrated impulsive action, immediate pleasure, and sexual experimentation

IV. The Freedom Movement
  A. Origins of the Movement
    1. The causes of the civil rights movement were many
  B. Separate and Unequal
    1. The United States in the 1950s was still a segregated, unequal society
    2. Few white Americans felt any urgency about confronting racial inequality
  C. The Legal Assault of Segregation
    1. It fell to the courts to confront the problem of racial segregation
      a. League of United Latin American Citizens (LULAC)
      b. Earl Warren
    2. For years, the NAACP, under the leadership of attorney Thurgood Marshall, had pressed legal challenges to the "separate but equal" doctrine laid down by the Supreme Court in 1896 in *Plessy v. Ferguson*
  D. *Brown v. Board of Education*
    1. Marshall brought the NAACP's support to local cases that had arisen when black parents challenged unfair school policies
  E. Warren's Decision
    1. Marshall argued that segregation did lifelong damage to black children, undermining their self-esteem
    2. Earl Warren managed to create unanimity on a divided Court, some of whose members disliked segregation but feared that a decision to outlaw it would spark widespread violence
    3. The black press hailed the *Brown* decision as a "second Emancipation Proclamation"
  F. The Montgomery Boycott
    1. *Brown* ensured that when the movement resumed after waning in the early 1950s it would have the backing of the federal courts
      a. Rosa Parks
      b. Bus boycott
  G. The Daybreak of Freedom
    1. The Montgomery bus boycott marked a turning point in postwar American history
      a. Nonviolent movement

        b. Gained northern support

        c. Established Martin Luther King, Jr., as the movement's national symbol

     2. From the beginning, the language of freedom pervaded the black movement

  H. The Leadership of King

     1. In King's soaring oratory, the protesters' understandings of freedom fused into a coherent whole

     2. A master at appealing to the deep sense of injustice among blacks and to the conscience of white America, King presented the case for black rights in a vocabulary that merged the black experience with that of the nation

     3. Echoing Christian themes derived from his training in the black church, King's speeches resonated deeply in both black communities and the broader culture

  I. Massive Resistance

     1. In 1956 King formed the Southern Christian Leadership Conference

     2. In 1956 many southern congressmen and senators signed a Southern Manifesto

  J. Eisenhower and Civil Rights

     1. The federal government tried to remain aloof from the black struggle

        a. President Eisenhower failed to provide moral leadership

     2. In 1957 Governor Orville Faubus of Arkansas used the National Guard to prevent the court-ordered integration of Little Rock's Central High School

        a. Eisenhower

V. The Election of 1960

  A. The Nomination of Kennedy

     1. The presidential campaign of 1960 turned out to be one of the closest in American history

     2. John F. Kennedy was a Catholic and the youngest presidential candidate in history

  B. Kennedy's Election

     1. Both Kennedy and Nixon were ardent Cold Warriors

        a. Missile gap

        b. Television debate

     2. Eisenhower's Farewell Address warned against the drumbeat of calls for a new military buildup

        a. Military-industrial complex

## SUGGESTED DISCUSSION QUESTIONS

- Describe how Bill Levitt and the GI Bill provided the opportunity for many Americans to buy the American Dream.

- Discuss the role of the family in both the fight against the Cold War and as part of new definition of freedom centered on consumerism.
- Explain residential segregation. How and why did cities become mostly black and suburbs mostly white? What were the consequences of such demographic patterns?
- Discuss modern Republicanism. Why, as the first Republican since Hoover, didn't Eisenhower dismantle the New Deal?
- How did Eisenhower continue the policy of containment set during the Truman Administration when fighting the Cold War? How was his policy the same as Truman's? How was it different?

## SUPPLEMENTAL WEB AND VISUAL RESOURCES

The Golden Age: 1950s
*dewey.chs.chico.k12.ca.us/decs5.html*
This site has a variety of options for researching the lifestyle of the 1950s in the United States.

*West Side Story*
*video.lowpriced.net/0792837614.html*
The classic movie, *West Side Story* is rated and available for purchase on this Web site.

President Eisenhower
*history.cc.ukans.edu/heritage/abilene/ikectr.html*
This site is produced by the Eisenhower Center and contains many links to information on topics ranging from Eisenhower's presidency to his family life.

Martin Luther King, Jr.
*www.stanford.edu/group/King/*
This is a helpful site produced by Stanford University focusing on the life of Martin Luther King, Jr., with multimedia features.

Communism
*www.films.com/Films_Home/item.cfm?s=1&bin=6459*
From the series, "History of the Twentieth Century," communism is documented from 1917 to 1991, focusing on the Soviets and Chinese in particular.

## SUPPLEMENTAL PRINT RESOURCES

Chappell, David. "A Stone of Hope: Prophetic Faith, Liberalism, and the Death of Jim Crow." *The Journal of The Historical Society* 3 no. 2 (2003): 129–62.
Divine, Robert. *The Sputnik Challenge: Eisenhower's Response to the Soviet Satellite.* New York: Oxford University Press, 1993.

Fraser, Cary. "Crossing the Color Line in Little Rock: The Eisenhower Administration and the Dilemma of Race for U.S. Foreign Policy." *Diplomatic History* 24, no. 2 (2000): 233–64.

Halberstam, David. *The Fifties*. New York: Villard Books, 1993.

Hodgson, Godfrey. *America in Our Time: From WWII to Nixon. What Happened and Why*. New York: Vintage, 1976.

Marling, Karal Ann. *As Seen on TV: The Visual Culture of Everyday Life in the 1950s*. Cambridge: Harvard University Press, 1994.

Meyerowitz, Joanne. "Beyond the Feminine Mystique: A Reassessment of Post-War Mass Culture, 1946–1958." *Journal of American History* 79, no. 4 (1993): 1455–82.

Pells, Richard. *The Liberal Mind in a Conservative Age: American Intellectuals in the 1940s and 1950s*. Middletown, CT: Wesleyan University Press, 1989.

Watson, Steven. *The Birth of the Beat Generation: Visionaries, Rebels, and Hipsters, 1944–1960*. New York: Pantheon, 1995.

Winkler, Allan. *Life Under a Cloud: American Anxiety About the Atom*. Champaign: University of Illinois Press, 1993.

## TEST BANK

### Matching

| | | |
|---|---|---|
| c | 1. Thurgood Marshall | a. *The Affluent Society* |
| f | 2. Jack Kerouac | b. "Checkers speech" |
| h | 3. William Levitt | c. chief justice of the Supreme Court |
| i | 4. Ho Chi Minh | d. founder of McDonalds |
| g | 5. David Riesman | e. NAACP lawyer |
| j | 6. John F. Kennedy | f. Beat writer |
| c | 7. Earl Warren | g. *The Lonely Crowd* |
| a | 8. John K. Galbraith | h. builder of suburbia |
| b | 9. Richard Nixon | i. Vietnamese leader |
| d | 10. Ray Kroc | j. Catholic presidential candidate |

| | | |
|---|---|---|
| d | 1. Southern Manifesto | a. residential racial segregation |
| c | 2. SCLC | b. active agent of social change |
| h | 3. social contract | c. coalition of black minister and activists |
| f | 4. free enterprise | d. denounced *Brown* as an abuse of judicial power |
| g | 5. Eisenhower Doctrine | e. Eisenhower's term for his policies |
| j | 6. *Brown v. Board of Education* | f. consumer capitalism |

a    7. blockbusting

b    8. Warren Court

e    9. modern Republicanism

i    10. Montgomery bus boycott

g. American pledge to help Middle Eastern countries

h. agreement between unions and employers

i. propelled Martin Luther King, Jr., as a national symbol

j. reversed the "separate but equal" doctrine

## Multiple Choice

1. The kitchen-debates were between
   a. Eisenhower and Nixon
   b. Nixon and Kennedy
   c. Eisenhower and Khrushchev
   *d. Khrushchev and Nixon
   e. Kennedy and Johnson

2. By 1960, approximately what percentage of Americans enjoyed the government-defined middle-class standard of living?
   a. 20 percent
   b. 35 percent
   c. 50 percent
   *d. 60 percent
   e. 80 percent

3. What was not a new innovation of the 1950s that helped to transform Americans' daily lives?
   a. jet air travel
   *b. electric iron
   c. television
   d. air conditioning
   e. automatic dishwasher

4. Which statement about industry is false?
   *a. The West did not benefit from the industries that sprang up from the Cold War
   b. By the mid-1950s white-collar workers outnumbered blue-collar factory and manual laborers
   c. Union's very success in raising wages inspired employers to mechanize more and more elements of manufacturing in order to reduce labor costs
   d. Since the 1950s, the American economy has shifted away from manufacturing
   e. New England benefited from the growth in the construction of aircraft engines and submarines

5. What state saw the greatest population increase between World War II and 1975?
   a. Arizona
   b. Washington
   c. Michigan
   d. Nevada
   *e. California

6. By the end of the 1950s, how many American families owned a TV set?
   a. 20 percent
   b. 35 percent
   c. 50 percent
   d. 75 percent
   *e. 90 percent

7. Along with a home and a TV, what became part of the "standard consumer package" of the 1950s?
   a. education
   b. record player
   *c. car
   d. credit card
   e. computer

8. Working women in the 1950s
   a. took industry jobs
   b. were applauded by society
   c. earned the same as men
   *d. worked part time for extra disposable income
   e. used their jobs as a vehicle for personal fulfillment

9. Dwight Eisenhower appointed what kind of individuals to his cabinet?
   a. the "Best and the Brightest"—young intellectuals in their fields
   b. former government men who had lots of combined political experience
   *c. wealthy businessmen, to run the government like an efficient business
   d. a balanced mixture of Republicans and Democrats since his party did not control Congress
   e. weak men with little experience so that he could have complete control over domestic and foreign affairs

10. Fearful that nationalist forces were really the work of Soviet Communists, Eisenhower frequently intervened in Third World countries. Which country did Eisenhower *not* get involved with during his administration?
    a. Iran
    b. Guatemala
    c. Vietnam
    d. Egypt
    *e. Angola

11. Which statement best describes the thesis of David Riesman's book *The Lonely Crowd*?
    a. White America had alienated black Americans from mainstream society
    *b. Americans were conformists and lacked the inner resources to lead truly independent lives
    c. Women were unhappy with the roles of wife and mother and longed for acceptance in higher education and other intellectual pursuits
    d. After World War II, Europe was left behind economically and politically with the emergence of the United States and Soviet Union as superpowers
    e. Unionism in America was doomed to fail if the union leaders did not embrace the fact that their demands and their strikes labeled them as Communists

12. Cultural life during the 1950s seemed more daring than the politics of the day. Which is not an example of 1950s cultural dissent?
    a. rock and roll
    b. *Playboy*
    *c. Port Huron Statement
    d. the Beats
    e. *The Catcher in the Rye*

13. What caused the civil rights movement of the 1950s?
    a. the mass migration out of the South to the North, beginning in World War I
    b. the destabilization of the racial system during World War II
    c. the Cold War, which demanded that the rhetoric of democracy be practiced in America
    d. the rise of independent states in the Third World
    *e. all of the above

14. Which vehicle was used most effectively for initializing institutional change during the civil rights movement in the 1950s?
    a. the Democratic Party
    b. the Executive branch
    c. the Republican Party
    *d. the Supreme Court
    e. the Legislative branch

15. Who argued the case *Brown v. Board of Education* before the Supreme Court?
    a. Fred Vinson
    *b. Thurgood Marshall
    c. Earl Warren
    d. Charles Darrow
    e. Martin Luther King, Jr.

16. What Supreme Court decision did *Brown* overturn?
    *a. *Plessy v. Ferguson*
    b. *Muller v. Oregon*
    c. *Yick Wo v. Hopkins*
    d. *Roe v. Wade*
    e. *Lochner v. New York*

17. The Montgomery bus boycott
    a. was sparked when Rosa Parks was arrested for refusing to give her seat up to a white man
    b. was successful in desegregating the public buses
    c. propelled Martin Luther King, Jr., into the national spotlight as a leader in the civil rights movement
    d. demonstrated that when the black community mobilized, it could defeat Jim Crow
    *e. all of the above

18. What organization did Martin Luther King, Jr., establish?
    a. SNCC
    b. CORE
    *c. SCLC
    d. NAACP
    e. Urban League

19. Which statement best describes how the white South reacted to the *Brown v. Board of Education* decision?
    a. It responded with extreme violence, typically burning down schools rather than integrating
    b. While the general public was outraged, southern congressional politicians supported the Supreme Court's decisions
    c. It worked closely with the NAACP, cooperating when it could to integrate schools
    *d. Some states closed the public schools rather than integrate, and offered white children the choice to opt out of integrated schools
    e. It took segregation in stride, recognizing that the time had come for change

20. Who warned against the dangerous powers of the "military-industrial complex"?
    a. Richard Nixon
    *b. Dwight Eisenhower
    c. John F. Kennedy
    d. Adlai Stevenson
    e. John Foster Dulles

## True or False

F  1. The kitchen-debates refer to the public debate during the 1950s regarding whether or not women ought to work outside the home.

T  2. Despite talk of the glories of the free market, government policies played a crucial role in the postwar economic boom.

T  3. The percentage of families at or below the poverty rate fell during the 1950s.

T  4. During the 1950s, the South became the home of numerous military bases and government-funded shipyards.

F  5. Although suburban communities were segregated in the 1950s, today, communities such as Levittown on Long Island are completely racially integrated.

T  6. The "standard consumer package" of the 1950s included a car, house, and television.

F  7. The 1950s was a decade of yet another radical movement of feminism, demanding equal rights as Alice Paul had presented them in the 1920s with her Equal Rights Amendment.

F  8. As residue from the Red Scare, anti-Semitism was widespread in America during the 1950s.

T  9. During the 1950s, religion had less to do with spiritual activities or sacred values than with personal identity and group assimilation.

F  10. The 1956 election brought landslide victories for the Republican Party, winning the White House and the Senate.

F  11. While in office, President Dwight Eisenhower rolled back the New Deal programs put forth by Franklin Roosevelt and Harry Truman.

T  12. Massive Retaliation was a policy that declared that any Soviet attack on an American ally would be countered by a nuclear assault on the Soviet Union itself.

F  13. The Eisenhower Doctrine was a promise to roll back communism in Eastern Europe.

F  14. Ngo Dinh Diem was a Buddhist with sympathy for the small farmers of South Vietnam and was thus America's choice to lead that country after the Geneva Conference.

T  15. The emergence of a popular culture geared to the emerging youth market suggested that significant generational tensions lay beneath the bland surface of 1950s life.

T    16. Thurgood Marshall argued before the Supreme Court in *Brown v. Board of Education* that segregation did lifelong damage to black children, undermining their self-esteem.

F    17. In a classic example of strong leadership, President Eisenhower convinced the American people that the *Brown* decision was the correct decision and a good decision for the sake of the country.

F    18. The Little Rock Central High School desegregation case established Martin Luther King, Jr., as the civil rights movement's national symbol.

T    19. Echoing Christian themes derived from his training in the black church, Martin Luther King, Jr.'s speeches resonated deeply in black southern communities.

F    20. In the 1960 presidential election John F. Kennedy defeated Richard Nixon by a landslide.

## Short Answer

*Identify and give the historical significance of each of the following terms, events, and people in a paragraph or two.*

1. consumer culture
2. modern Republicanism
3. Martin Luther King, Jr.
4. Third World
5. role for women
6. automobile
7. *Brown v. Board of Education*
8. suburbs
9. Rosa Parks
10. Nikita Khrushchev

## Essay Questions

1. Discuss the changes in the American economy during the postwar period. Be sure to discuss the agricultural, industrial, and consumer sectors of the economy.

2. The Nixon-Khrushchev debates held in the setting of a suburban kitchen illustrated how freedom in America had come to mean economic abundance and consumer choices during the 1950s. Write an essay that demonstrates this definition of freedom and explains the historical significance of those debates.

3. Thinking back to the chapter on the 1920s, compare and contrast the consumerism of that decade with the 1950s. How did the economic prosperity of each decade affect the meaning Americans gave to freedom?

4. *House Beautiful* magazine stated that the country's most powerful weapon in the Cold War was "the freedom offered by washing machines and dishwashers, vacuum cleaners, automobiles, and refrigerators." Analyze this

statement, explaining how consumerism was used in the 1950s to combat the Cold War. Is consumerism used today as a tool of American foreign policy?

5. Explain the role of women in 1950s American society. What were women expected to do? What kind of work did they perform? How was this idealized lifestyle supposed to be a weapon in the Cold War? Be sure to use Richard Nixon's "kitchen-debate" in your answer, as well as the idea that the home became the center of freedom.

6. American foreign policies in Third World countries were determined by Cold War doctrine. Explain American foreign policy in the Third World during the Eisenhower Administration. Be sure to discuss Iran, Guatemala, and Vietnam.

7. Historian Carl Degler titled his book on the years 1945–1966 *The Age of Affluence and Anxiety*. Thinking back to the previous chapter as well, does this title accurately portray the paradox of the 1950s? Why, or why not?

8. The civil rights movement gained momentum in the 1950s, nearly ninety years after Reconstruction. Explain why the movement finally took off in the 1950s. What caused it to do so? Be sure to think back to previous chapters.

9. Martin Luther King, Jr., becomes the perfect leader for the civil rights movement in the South. Defend this statement by explaining what he brought to the movement. Be sure to employ the *Voices of Freedom* excerpt in your answer.

**CHAPTER 25** | The Sixties, 1960–1968

This chapter concentrates on the history of the 1960s, with emphasis on the civil rights movement, the Great Society program, and the war in Vietnam. The chapter opens with the sit-in movement of 1960, demonstrating the growing frustration over the slow pace of change. As the decade progressed, the civil rights movement grew with grassroots organizations and substantial student participation. The Freedom Rides, Birmingham, and the March on Washington are explored, revealing the core demands of the movement. The Kennedy years are looked at next, discussing JFK's foreign policy, the Peace Corps, Alliance for Progress, and the Cuban Missile Crisis. After Kennedy's assassination, Lyndon Johnson immediately worked to get the Civil Rights Act through Congress. Following that, the civil rights movement rallied around the Freedom Summer, Johnson's 1964 election campaign, and the passage of the Voting Rights Act. Genuinely concerned about civil rights, Johnson launched his Great Society program, enlarging the freedoms begun during the New Deal. By mid-decade, the civil rights movement moved North and urban ghettos were plagued by riots. Appealing to the concerns of the northern black urban communities were Malcolm X and the idea of Black Power. Both the civil rights movement and the Great Society become overshadowed by the war in Vietnam. Determined to change society and ensure freedom as participatory democracy, the Students for a Democratic Society issued the Port Huron Statement, highlighted in *Voices of Freedom,* and headed the antiwar movement. As the 1960s progressed, young Americans' understanding of freedom expanded to include cultural freedom as well, as seen with the counterculture. Next, the chapter looks at the other movements of the 1960s, including the feminist, gay, Latino, Indian, environmental, and consumer rights movements. The liberal Warren Court is discussed too, as it extended many rights in the 1960s. Finally, the chapter concludes with the turbulent events of 1968, beginning with the Tet Offensive and culminating with the election of Richard Nixon.

## CHAPTER OUTLINE

I. Greensboro Sit-in

II. The Freedom Movement
    A. The Rising Tide of Protest
        1. CORE organized the Freedom Rides in 1961
        2. As protests escalated so did the resistance of local authorities
          a. Albany, Georgia
          b. James Meredith
    B. Birmingham
        1. The high point of protest came in the spring of 1963
        2. Martin Luther King, Jr., led a demonstration in Birmingham, Alabama
          a. *Letter from Birmingham Jail*
        3. King made the bold decision to send black school children into the streets of Birmingham
          a. Bull Connor unleashed his forces against the children
        4. The events in Birmingham forced white Americans to decide whether they had more in common with fellow citizens demanding their basic rights or with violent segregationists
          a. Medgar Evers
    C. The March on Washington
        1. The March on Washington was organized by a coalition of civil rights, labor, and church organizations led by A. Philip Randolph
        2. The March on Washington reflected an unprecedented degree of black-white cooperation in support of racial and economic justice while reveling some of the movement's limitations, and the tensions within it

III. The Kennedy Years
    A. Kennedy and the World
        1. Kennedy's agenda envisioned new initiatives aimed at countering communist influence in the world
          a. Peace Corps
          b. Space program
        2. Kennedy's Alliance for Progress was aimed at Latin America
    B. The Bay of Pigs
        1. Kennedy failed at ousting Castro from power in Cuba
    C. The Missile Crisis
        1. The most dangerous crisis of the Kennedy administration came in October 1962, when American spy planes discovered that the Soviet Union was installing missiles in Cuba capable of reaching the United States with nuclear weapons

2. In 1963, Kennedy moved to reduce Cold War tensions
   a. Limited Test-Ban Treaty
  D. Kennedy and Civil Rights
    1. Kennedy failed to protect civil rights workers from violence, insisting that law enforcement was a local matter
    2. The events in Birmingham in 1963 forced Kennedy to take more action
  E. The Assassination
    1. Kennedy was shot on November 22, 1963, in Dallas

IV. Lyndon Johnson's Presidency
  A. Civil Rights under Johnson
    1. Immediately after becoming president, Lyndon Johnson identified himself with the black movement more passionately than any previous president
    2. In 1964, Congress passed the Civil Rights Act
  B. Freedom Summer
    1. The 1964 law did not address a major concern of the civil rights movement—the right to vote in the South
    2. Freedom Summer was a voter registration drive in Mississippi
      a. Schwerner, Goodman, and Chaney
    3. Freedom Summer led directly to the campaign by the Mississippi Freedom Democratic Party (MFDP)
      a. Fannie Lou Hammer
  C. The 1964 Election
    1. Lyndon B. Johnson's opponent was Barry Goldwater, who was portrayed as pro–nuclear war and anti–civil rights
    2. Johnson was stigmatized by the Democrats as an extremist who would repeal Social Security and risk nuclear war
    3. Proposition 14 repealed a 1963 law banning racial discrimination in the sale of real estate
  D. Selma and Voting Rights
    1. In 1965 King led a group in a march from Selma to Montgomery
    2. The federal government took action when there was violence against nonviolent demonstrators
      a. 1965 Voting Rights Act
      b. Twenty-fourth Amendment
  E. Immigration Reform
    1. The belief that racism should no longer serve as a basis of public policy spilled over into other realms
    2. Taken together, the civil rights revolution and immigration reform marked the triumph of a pluralist conception of Americanism
  F. The Great Society
    1. Johnson outlined the most sweeping proposal for governmental action to promote the general welfare since the New Deal

2. Unlike the New Deal, however, the Great Society was a response to prosperity, not depression

G. The War on Poverty
  1. The centerpiece of the Great Society crusade to eradicate poverty
    a. Michael Harrington's *The Other America*
  2. In the 1960s, the administration attributed poverty to an absence of skills and a lack of proper attitudes and work habits
  3. The War on Poverty concentrated on equipping the poor with skills and rebuilding their spirit and motivation
    a. Office of Economic Opportunity

H. Freedom and Equality
  1. Johnson resurrected the phrase "freedom from want," all but forgotten during the 1950s
  2. Johnson's Great Society may not have achieved equality "as a fact," but it represented a remarkable reaffirmation of the idea of social citizenship
  3. Coupled with the decade's high rate of economic growth, the War on Poverty succeeded in reducing the incidence of poverty from 22 percent to 13 percent of American families during the 1960s

V. The Changing Black Movement
  A. The Ghetto Uprising
    1. In 1965 a Watts uprising left 35 dead, 900 injured and $30 million in property damage
    2. By the summer of 1967, violence had become so widespread that some feared racial civil war
      a. Kerner Report
  B. Economic Freedom
    1. With black unemployment twice that of whites and average black family income little more than half the white norm, the movement looked for ways to "make freedom real" for black Americans
      a. "Bill of Rights for the Disadvantaged"
      b. Freedom Budget
    2. In 1966, King launched the Chicago Freedom Movement, with demands quite different from its predecessors in the South
      a. The movement failed
  C. Malcolm X
    1. Malcolm X had insisted that blacks must control the political and economic resources of their communities and rely on their own efforts rather than working with whites
    2. After a trip to Mecca, Malcolm X began to speak of the possibility of interracial cooperation for radical change in the United States
  D. The Rise of Black Power
    1. Black Power immediately became a rallying cry for those bitter over the federal government's failure to stop violence against civil rights

workers, white attempts to determine movement strategy, and the civil rights movement's failure to have any impact on the economic problems of black ghettos

2. The idea reflected the radicalization of young civil rights activists and sparked and explosion of racial self-assertion
3. Inspired by the idea of black self-determination, SNCC and CORE repudiated their previous interracialism and new militant groups sprang into existence
   a. Black Panther Party

VI. Vietnam and the New Left
   A. Old and New Lefts
      1. What made the New Left new was its rejection of the intellectual and political categories that had shaped radicalism for most of the twentieth century
      2. The New Left was not as new as it claimed
      3. The New Left's greatest inspiration was the black freedom movement
   B. Participatory Democracy
      1. The years 1962 and 1963 witnessed the appearance of several pathbreaking books that challenged one aspect or another of the 1950s consensus
      2. The Port Huron Statement offered a new vision of social change
         a. Freedom meant "participatory democracy"
   C. The Free Speech Movement
      1. In 1964, events at the University of California at Berkeley revealed the possibility for a far broader mobilization of students in the name of participatory democracy
         a. Mario Savio
   D. America and Vietnam
      1. The war in Vietnam transformed student protest into a full-fledged generational rebellion
      2. Fear that the public would not forgive them for "losing" Vietnam made it impossible for Presidents Kennedy and Johnson to remove the United States from an increasingly untenable situation
   E. Lyndon Johnson's War
      1. Congress passed the Gulf of Tonkin resolution in 1964, authorizing the president to take "all necessary measures to repel armed attack" in Vietnam
      2. Although Johnson campaigned in 1964 against sending U.S. troops to Vietnam, troops arrived in 1965
      3. By 1968, the number of American troops in Vietnam exceeded half a million and the conduct of the war had become more and more brutal
   F. Critics of the War
      1. As casualties mounted and American bombs poured down on North

and South Vietnam, the Cold War foreign policy consensus began to unravel
2. Opposition to the war became the organizing theme that united all kinds of doubts and discontents
  a. The burden of fighting fell on the working class and the poor
G. The Antiwar Movement
  1. SDS began antiwar demonstrations in 1965
    a. Carl Ogelsby
H. The Counterculture
  1. As the 1960s progressed, young Americans' understanding of freedom expanded to include cultural freedom
 I. Liberation
  1. Liberation was a massive redefinition of freedom as a rejection of all authority
  2. The counterculture in some ways represented not rebellion but the fulfillment of the consumer marketplace
  3. To young dissenters, personal liberation represented a spirit of creative experimentation, a search for a way of life in which friendship and pleasure eclipsed the single-minded pursuit of wealth
  4. The counterculture emphasized the ideal of community
  5. The counterculture's notion of liberation centered on the free individual
    a. Sexual freedom

VII. The New Movements and the Rights Revolution
A. The Reawakening of Feminism
B. The Feminine Mystique
  1. The public reawakening of feminist consciousness came with the publication in 1963 of Betty Friedan's *The Feminine Mystique*
  2. The immediate result of *The Feminine Mystique* was to focus attention on yet another gap between American rhetoric and American reality
  3. The law slowly began to address feminist concerns
  4. 1966 saw the formation of the National Organization for Women (NOW), with Friedan as president
C. Women's Liberation
  1. Many women in the civil rights movement concluded that the treatment of women in society was not much better than society's treatment of blacks
  2. The same complaints arose in SDS
  3. By 1967, women throughout the country were establishing "consciousness-raising" groups to discuss the sources of their discontent

      4. The new feminism burst onto the national scene at the Miss America beauty pageant of 1968

        a. "bra-burners"

  D. Personal Freedom

      1. Women believed that "the personal is political," thus permanently changing Americans' definition of freedom

      2. Radical feminists' first public campaign demanded the repeal of state laws that underscored women's lack of self-determination by banning abortions or leaving it up to physicians to decide whether a pregnancy could be terminated

  E. Gay Liberation

      1. Gay men and lesbians had long been stigmatized as sinful or mentally disordered

      2. The 1960s transformed the gay movement

        a. Stonewall Bar

  F. Latino Activism

      1. The movement emphasized pride in both the Mexican past and the new Chicano culture that had arisen in the United States

        a. Cesar Chavez

      2. In New York City, the Young Lords Organization modeled on the Black Panthers staged street demonstrations to protest the high unemployment rate among the city's Puerto Ricans and the lack of city services in Latino neighborhoods

  G. Red Power

      1. Indian activists demanded not simply economic aid but also greater self-determination

        a. American Indian Movement

        b. Indians of All Nations

        c. Red Power movement

  H. The New Environmentalism

      1. The new environmentalism was more activist and youth-oriented, and spoke the language of empowering citizens to participate in decisions that affected their lives

      2. Rachel Carson's *Silent Spring* spurred the movement

      3. Despite vigorous opposition from business groups that considered its proposals a violation of property rights, environmentalism attracted the broadest bipartisan support of any of the new social movements

        a. April 22, 1970—Earth Day

  I. Consumer Activism

      1. Closely related to environmentalism was the consumer movement, spearheaded by the lawyer Ralph Nader

  J. The Rights Revolution

      1. Under the guidance of Chief Justice Earl Warren, the Supreme Court vastly expanded the rights enjoyed by all Americans

2. The Court moved to rein in the anticommunist crusade in 1957 on what is known as "Red Monday"
3. The Court continued to guard civil liberties in the 1950s and 1960s

K. Policing the States
   1. The Court simultaneously pushed forward the process of imposing upon the states the obligation to respect the liberties outlined in the Bill of Rights
      a. *Miranda v. Arizona*
      b. *Baker v. Carr*

L. The Right to Privacy
   1. The Warren Court outlined entirely new rights in response to the rapidly changing contours of American society
      a. *Griswold v. Connecticut*
      b. *Roe v. Wade*
   2. *Griswold* and *Roe* unleashed a flood of rulings and laws that seemed to accept the feminist view of the family as a collection of sovereign individuals rather than a unit with a single head

VIII. 1968
   A. A Year of Turmoil
      1. The 1960s reached their climax in 1968, a year when momentous events succeeded each other with such rapidity that the foundations of society seemed to be dissolving
         a. Tet Offensive
         b. LBJ withdrew from 1968 election
         c. Martin Luther King, Jr., was assassinated
         d. Columbia University student strike
         e. Robert Kennedy was assassinated
         f. Chicago Democratic National Convention
   B. Nixon's Comeback
      1. The year's events opened the door for a conservative reaction
      2. Richard Nixon campaigned as the champion of the "silent majority"
   C. The Legacy of the 1960s
      1. The 1960s produced new rights and a new understanding of freedom

## SUGGESTED DISCUSSION QUESTIONS

- Describe how the movements of the 1960s exposed the limitations of traditional New Deal liberalism.
- Describe how the movements of the 1960s forced a reconsideration of foreign policy.
- Discuss how the Great Society expanded the freedoms and liberties of Americans left out of Roosevelt's New Deal.

- Who was the New Left? How does their manifesto, The Port Huron Statement, define freedom and democracy in America? Why do you think they are so critical of American society and politics?
- What did the civil rights movement do to empower other minorities to fight for their rights? Of all the movements, which one had the most success? By 1968, are there any groups that are still left behind in achieving full freedom? Why?
- Evaluate the significance of Richard Nixon's 1968 victory.

## SUPPLEMENTAL WEB AND VISUAL RESOURCES

*Letter from the Birmingham Jail*
*almaz.com/nobel/peace/MLK-jail.html*
This site features Martin Luther King, Jr.'s letter in HTML and PDF format.

John F. Kennedy
*www.geocities.com/~newgeneration/index.html*
This site contains various resources such as speeches, pictures, videos, and a bibliography.

Vietnam
*www.pbs.org/wgbh/amex/vietnam/*
PBS's "American Experience" has created *Vietnam: A Television History* video series with a companion book to accompany it. The site is full of other resources for information pertaining to the Vietnam War.

Malcolm X
*www.brothermalcolm.net/*
This site contains information pertaining to the life of Malcolm X, including chronologies, speeches, and photographs.

Lyndon B. Johnson
*www.grolier.com/presidents/ea/bios/36pjohn.html*
This site has a helpful biography on Lyndon B. Johnson with links for further research.

Free Speech Movement
*bancroft.berkeley.edu/FSM/*
This site chronicles the Free Speech movement at Berkeley, including oral histories and primary documents.

## SUPPLEMENTAL PRINT RESOURCES

Bresler, Robert. *Us vs. Them: American Political and Cultural Conflict from WWII to Watergate.* Wilmington, DE: Scholarly Resources, 2000.

DeGroot, Gerard. *A Noble Cause? America and the Vietnam War*. New York: Longman, 2000.

Halberstam, David. *The Children*. New York: Random House, 1998.

Logevall, Fredrik. *Choosing War: The Lost Chance for Peace and the Escalation of War in Vietnam*. Berkeley: University of California Press, 1999.

Loss, Archie. *Pop Dreams: Music, Movies, and the Media in the 1960s*. New York: Harcourt Brace, 1999.

Moody, Anne. *Coming of Age in Mississippi*. New York: Dell, 1968.

Schwartz, Bernard, ed., *The Warren Court: A Retrospective*. New York: Oxford University Press, 1996.

Wells, Tom. *The War Within: America's Battle over Vietnam*. Berkeley: University of California Press, 1994.

Williamson, Joel. *A Rage for Order: Black-White Relations in the American South Since Emancipation*. New York: Oxford University Press, 1986.

## TEST BANK

### Matching

| | | | |
|---|---|---|---|
| e | 1. James Meredith | a. | Republican presidential candidate |
| h | 2. Michael Harrington | b. | SDS leader |
| g | 3. Fidel Castro | c. | *Letter from Birmingham Jail* |
| i | 4. Betty Friedan | d. | National Farm Workers' Association |
| j | 5. Malcolm X | e. | University of Mississippi |
| c | 6. Martin Luther King, Jr. | f. | supporter of Black Power movement |
| b | 7. Carl Ogelsby | g. | Bay of Pigs |
| d | 8. Cesar Chavez | h. | *The Other America* |
| a | 9. Barry Goldwater | i. | founder of NOW |
| f | 10. Stokely Carmichael | j. | Nation of Islam |

| | | | |
|---|---|---|---|
| h | 1. Peace Corps | a. | SDS |
| f | 2. Freedom Summer | b. | Richard Nixon's voter base |
| e | 3. *New York Times v. Sullivan* | c. | a congressional "blank check" |
| b | 4. silent majority | d. | outlawed the poll-tax |
| i | 5. Alliance for Progress | e. | freedom of the press |
| a | 6. Port Huron Statement | f. | voter registration drive |
| d | 7. Twenty-fourth Amendment | g. | protection for abortion |
| g | 8. *Roe v. Wade* | h. | young American volunteers to help abroad |
| j | 9. *Silent Spring* | i. | aid for Latin America |
| c | 10. Gulf of Tonkin resolution | j. | environmental movement |

## Multiple Choice

1. The sit-in at Greensboro, North Carolina, in 1960
   *a. reflected the mounting frustration at the slow pace of racial change
   b. was the last of a series of violent agitations for civil rights in 1960
   c. had no real effect on the momentum of the civil rights movement
   d. was largely organized by members of King's SCLC
   e. illustrated how civil rights activists embraced the violent messages of Malcolm X

2. Freedom Riders were
   a. welcomed by white southerners
   b. never arrested
   c. only black students
   *d. attacked by the local KKK
   e. unsuccessful in their efforts

3. Martin Luther King, Jr.'s *Letter from Birmingham Jail* declared that
   a. the civil rights movement had become too violent and had to stop
   *b. the white moderate had to put aside his fear of disorder and commit to racial justice
   c. the federal government was solely responsible for the violence in the South
   d. the white clergy in the South had done a tremendous job fighting Jim Crow
   e. he was abandoning his policy of civil disobedience and peaceful demonstration

4. The goal of the March on Washington was
   a. passage of a civil rights bill that was languishing in Congress
   b. a public works program to reduce unemployment
   c. a law barring discrimination in employment
   d. an increase in the minimum wage
   *e. all of the above

5. What event forced John F. Kennedy to take meaningful action in support of the civil rights movement?
   a. Selma to Birmingham March
   b. March on Washington rally
   *c. King's demonstrations in Birmingham
   d. Greensboro sit-ins
   e. Freedom Summer campaign

6. Republican Barry Goldwater viewed _____ as an "internal danger to freedom."
   *a. the New Deal welfare state
   b. the nuclear weapons buildup

   c. the military-industrial complex
   d. the proliferation of private charities
   e. the Warren Court

7. The 1964 Civil Rights Act did not
   a. prohibit racial discrimination in employment
   b. ban discrimination on the grounds of sex
   *c. ban discriminatory laws that prevented suffrage
   d. prohibit racial discrimination in privately owned public
      accommodations
   e. prohibit racial discrimination in institutions like hospitals and schools

8. Johnson's administration attributed poverty in America to all of the
   following except
   a. poor work habits
   *b. flawed economic institutions
   c. an absence of skills
   d. past injustice and prejudice
   e. a lack of proper attitudes

9. Which statement about the Immigration Reform Act of 1965 is correct?
   a. The act tightened the quotas set in 1924
   b. The act lifted the quotas set in 1924 and European immigration
      skyrocketed
   *c. The act lifted the quotas set in 1924 and European immigration decreased
   d. The act was forced through Congress in response to increasing
      Vietnamese refugees
   e. The act had no recognizable impact on immigration patterns

10. The Chicago Freedom movement launched by Martin Luther King, Jr., in
    1966 fought for
    a. an end to discrimination by employers and unions
    b. equal access to mortgages
    c. integration of public housing
    d. construction of low-income housing
    *e. all of the above

11. Black Power emerged as a response to
    a. the frustrations over the federal government's failure to stop violence
       against civil rights workers
    b. white workers' attempts to determine the civil rights movement's
       strategy
    c. the civil rights movement's failure to have any impact on the economic
       problems of black ghettos
    d. the growing ideas of racial self-assertion and black self-determination
    *e. all of the above

12. Which statement about the New Left is true?
    a. the New Left were mostly black college students
    b. the New Left and the counterculture were the same thing
    *c. the New Left advocated for peace, civil rights, and economic equality
    d. the New Left were mostly children of the Old Right
    e. all of the above

13. What is the attitude of the New Left toward university professors as seen in the Port Huron Statement?
    a. They have tremendous respect for them
    *b. They believe that they are puppets of the military-industrial complex
    c. They see them as leaders in the antiwar movement
    d. They are skeptical of them since most professors were older than thirty
    e. They saw them as the bearers of liberal knowledge and reform

14. The National Organization for Women (NOW) campaigned for
    a. an end to the mass media's false image of women
    b. equal job opportunities for women
    c. equal educational opportunities
    d. equal opportunities in politics
    *e. all of the above

15. Rachel Carson's *Silent Spring* inspired what movement?
    *a. environmental movement
    b. feminist movement
    c. lesbian movement
    d. conservative movement
    e. Indian movement

16. The Warren Court
    a. was a conservative Court with the one exception of *Brown v Board of Education*
    *b. seemed to accept the feminist view of the family as a collection of sovereign individuals rather than a unit with a single male head
    c. began a trend to halt the liberal views that had begun in the late 1950s that government had an obligation to provide for the welfare of the citizens
    d. condemned Lyndon Johnson for abuses of power during the Vietnam War
    e. was praised by 1968 Republican presidential candidate Richard Nixon

17. The civil rights movement inspired
    a. the feminist movement
    b. the Red Power movement
    c. the gay and lesbian movement
    d. the antiwar movement
    *e. all of the above

18. What event marked the turning point in the Vietnam conflict, forcing Lyndon Johnson to change courses and pull out of the upcoming presidential race?
  *a. the Tet Offensive
  b. Operation Rolling Thunder
  c. the invasion of Cambodia
  d. the Gulf of Tonkin
  e. revelations about the My Lai massacre

19. What event did not occur in 1968?
  a. Robert Kennedy's assassination
  b. riots outside the Democratic National Convention
  c. the assassination of Martin Luther King, Jr.
  *d. the assassination of Medgar Evers
  e. the Tet Offensive in Vietnam

20. Richard Nixon appealed to what group in his 1968 election campaign?
  a. the Moral Majority
  b. the New Left
  c. the Progressive-Republicans
  d. the new feminists
  *e. the silent majority

## True or False

T    1. The movements of the 1960s challenged the 1950s understanding of freedom linked to the Cold War abroad and consumer choice at home.

F    2. The violence in Birmingham was surprising since it was a relatively peaceful city with little history of racial conflict.

T    3. The slogan of the March on Washington was "Jobs and Freedom."

F    4. John F. Kennedy was staunchly committed to civil rights and he placed it as his number one priority in his inaugural address.

F    5. John F. Kennedy's foreign policy for Latin America, called Alliance for Progress, was a huge success.

F    6. The Cuban Missile Crisis did nothing to change Kennedy's attitude toward the Cold War.

T    7. Lyndon Johnson held the New Deal view that government had an obligation to assist the less fortunate members of society.

T    8. Johnson defeated Barry Goldwater by a landslide in 1964.

F    9. The Freedom Summer refers to the summer of 1968 when the Democrats rallied around the campaign of Robert Kennedy.

F    10. The Immigration Reform Act did not alter the rate or national origin of immigration after 1965.

T    11. Coupled with the decade's high rate of economic growth, the War on Poverty succeeded in reducing the incidence of poverty from 22 percent to 13 percent of American families during the 1960s.

T    12. The Kerner Report blamed ghetto violence on segregation and poverty.

T    13. As Martin Luther King, Jr., came to realize the difficulty of combating the economic plight of black America, King's language became more and more radical.

F    14. The New Left took for its model the Soviet Union and viewed the working class as the main agent of social change.

T    15. The Port Huron Statement offered a new vision of social change while defining freedom to mean "participatory democracy."

F    16. Congress passed the Gulf of Tonkin resolution in 1964 by a very narrow margin, authorizing the president to take "all necessary measures to repel armed attack" in Vietnam.

T    17. During the feminist movement, women came to believe that "the personal is political," thus permanently changing Americans' definition of freedom.

T    18. As a result of the Red Power movement, many more Americans began to identify themselves as Indians than before 1960.

T    19. Despite vigorous opposition from business groups that considered its proposals a violation of property rights, environmentalism attracted the broadest bipartisan support of any of the new social movements.

F    20. Under the guidance of Chief Justice Earl Warren, the Supreme Court vastly contracted the rights enjoyed by all Americans in the 1960s.

## Short Answer

*Identify and give the historical significance of each of the following terms, events, and people in a paragraph or two.*

1. Freedom Summer
2. Port Huron Statement
3. Betty Friedan
4. Cuban Missile Crisis
5. Warren Court

6. Martin Luther King, Jr.
7. Tet Offensive
8. Great Society
9. Black Power
10. Civil Rights Act (1964)

## Essay Questions

1. During the 1960s, the United States had become a more open, more tolerant—in a word, freer—country. Defend or refute that statement.

2. Assess how important the federal government was in the 1950s and 1960s in the civil rights movement compared to how important the student movement was in affecting social change. How necessary was the federal government? How eager and responsive was it? Why did the government stand on the sidelines or get actively involved?

3. Comment on what James Baldwin said of the civil rights movement challenging the United States to rethink "what it really means by freedom"—including whether freedom applied to all Americans or only to part of the population.

4. How did John F. Kennedy's foreign policy agenda envision new initiatives aimed at countering communist influence in the world? How successful was Kennedy's foreign policy?

5. Compare Lyndon Johnson's Great Society with Franklin Roosevelt's New Deal. Be sure to discuss how the Great Society was a response to prosperity unlike the New Deal, which was a response to depression.

6. Lyndon Johnson said that economic freedom meant more than equal opportunity. Explain what he meant by that statement and how his Great Society program attempted to bring economic freedom to all members of American society.

7. Explain why, at first glance, the cooperation between the New Left and the civil rights movement seemed an unlikely combination. Then describe what basic assumptions the two movements shared to make their partnership successful. Be sure to employ the *Voices of Freedom* excerpt.

8. Discuss how successful the antiwar movement was in changing the course of the war. What methods did it use? How did the movement view freedom and the war?

9. 1968 was a turbulent year. Describe the events of 1968 and their significance in both the civil rights movement and the antiwar movement.

10. Compare the civil rights movement in the South with that in the North. Be sure to discuss methods, leadership, and issues that were being addressed and the successes of each.

**CHAPTER 26**

# The Triumph of Conservatism, 1969–1988

This chapter concentrates on the history of the Nixon through the Reagan years, when conservatism prevailed in American politics and society. Opening with the 1964 presidential campaign of Barry Goldwater, the chapter illustrates the growing tide of conservatism in the 1960s. Similarly, looking at libertarians, "new conservatives," and the Young Americans for Freedom, one sees that there were conservative forces at work in the 1960s, along with the more liberal forces discussed in the previous chapter. Highlighting this is the Sharon Statement from the YAF in *Voices of Freedom*. Richard Nixon's domestic policies were not reflective of a staunch conservative agenda. His expansion of the welfare state and commitment to the environment surprised many conservatives. Likewise, Nixon approached the Cold War in a new way, reducing tensions between the United States and the communist world through a policy of détente. However, in the Third World American foreign policy remained committed to supporting pro-American dictatorships. The end of the Vietnam War came in 1973, but the Watergate scandal tarnished Nixon's foreign policy successes. Unable to withstand the spending of the 1960s, the increasing inflation, and the oil embargoes, the American economy stagnated in the 1970s while inflation soared. Neither Nixon, nor Gerald Ford, nor Jimmy Carter proved adequate at recovering the economy. Jimmy Carter's administration is examined next, highlighting his commitment to human rights in foreign policy. However, with a failing economy and a foreign policy that seemed weak to many Americans, Carter lost the 1980 election to Ronald Reagan. Reagan's election came on the rising tide of conservatism as seen through the Moral Majority, debates over the ERA, and the tax revolts. Reagan's economic policies, reductions in social programs and his foreign policy conclude the chapter.

## CHAPTER OUTLINE

I. Barry Goldwater

II. The Rebirth of Conservatism
   A. The Libertarians
      1. To "libertarian" conservatives, freedom meant individual autonomy, limited government, and unregulated capitalism
      2. These ideas had great appeal in the rapidly growing South and West
      3. Milton Friedman identified the free market as the necessary foundation for individual liberty
   B. The New Conservatism
      1. "New conservatism" became increasingly prominent in the 1950s
      2. Proponents insisted that toleration of difference offered no substitute for the search for absolute truth
      3. The "new conservatives" understood freedom as first and foremost a moral condition
      4. The conservative movement was divided between libertarians and "new conservatives"
      5. Two powerful enemies became focal points for the conservative revival
         a. The Soviet Union abroad
         b. The federal government at home
   C. The Conservative 1960s
      1. With the founding in 1960 of Young Americans for Freedom (YAF), conservative students emerged as a force in politics
         a. Sharon Statement
   D. Conservatism and Race
      1. The funds that poured into the Goldwater campaign from the Sun Belt's oilmen and aerospace entrepreneurs established a new financial base for conservatism
      2. A reaction against civil rights gains offered conservatives new opportunities and threatened the stability of the Democratic coalition
         a. "Southern strategy"

III. President Nixon
   A. Nixon's Domestic Policies
      1. Having won the presidency by a very narrow margin, Nixon moved toward the political center on many issues
      2. The Nixon administration created a host of new federal agencies
         a. EPA
         b. OSHA
         c. NTSB

        3. Nixon spent lavishly on social services and environmental initiatives
- B. Nixon and Welfare
    1. Perhaps Nixon's most startling initiative was his proposal for a Family Assistance Plan
        a. The plan would have replaced AFDC with a guaranteed annual income but failed in Congress
- C. Nixon and Race
    1. To consolidate support in the white South, Nixon nominated to the Supreme Court conservative southern jurists with records of support for segregation
        a. Both were rejected by the Senate
    2. The Nixon administration also pursued "affirmative action" programs to upgrade minority employment
        a. Philadelphia Plan
    3. Trade union of skilled workers strongly opposed the Philadelphia Plan
- D. The Burger Court
    1. Warren Burger was expected to lead the justices in a conservative direction but surprised many of his supporters
    2. In *Swann v. Charlotte-Mecklenburg Board of Education,* busing was used as a tool to achieve integration
        a. Boston
    3. In *San Antonio v. Rodriguez*, a 5-4 Court majority ruled that the Constitution did not require equality of school funding
- E. The Court and Affirmative Action
    1. Many whites came to view affirmative action programs as a form of "reverse discrimination"
    2. In *Bakke* the Court ruled that fixed quotas was unconstitutional but that race could be used as one factor among many in college admissions decisions
- F. The Continuing Sexual Revolution
    1. To the alarm of conservatives during the 1970s the sexual revolution passed from the counterculture into the social mainstream
    2. The figure for divorces in 1975 exceeded the number of first-time marriages
    3. Women made inroads into areas from which they had long been excluded in the 1970s
        a. Title IX
        b. Equal Credit Opportunity Act
        c. More employment opportunities
    4. The gay and lesbian movement expanded greatly during the 1970s and became a major concern of the Right

G. Nixon and Détente
　1. Conservatives viewed Nixon's foreign policy as dangerously "soft" on communism
　2. Nixon and Henry Kissinger continued their predecessors' policy of attempting to undermine governments deemed dangerous to American strategic or economic interests
　　a. Chile
　3. In his relation with the major Communist powers, however, Nixon fundamentally altered Cold War policies
　4. Nixon visited China in 1972
　5. Nixon then went to Moscow, signing SALT
　　a. Détente

IV. Vietnam and Watergate
　A. Nixon and Vietnam
　　1. Nixon ran for president in 1968, declaring that he had a "secret plan" to end the war
　　　a. Vietnamization
　　2. Antiwar protests climaxed in 1970
　　　a. Kent State and Jackson State Universities
　　3. Public support for the war was rapidly waning
　　　a. My Lai massacre
　　　b. War Powers Act of 1973
　B. The End of the Vietnam War
　　1. The Paris peace agreement made possible the final withdrawal of American troops in 1973
　　2. Vietnam was a military, political, and social disaster
　C. Watergate
　　1. Nixon was obsessed with secrecy and could not accept honest difference of opinion
　　　a. Pentagon Papers led to the "plumbers"
　　2. The Watergate break-in was covered up by the White House
　　　a. Nixon's tapes
　D. Nixon's Fall
　　1. In August 1974, the House Judiciary Committee voted to recommend that Nixon be impeached for conspiracy to obstruct justice
　　　a. Nixon resigned
　　2. Nixon's presidency remains a classic example of the abuse of political power
　　3. Frank Church led investigations against the CIA
　　　a. Church Committee revelations seriously undermined Americans' confidence in their own government

        4. Liberals, who had despised Nixon throughout his career, celebrated his downfall

           a. Foundations of liberalism were weakened

V. The End of the Golden Age

  A. The Decline of Manufacturing

    1. During the 1970s, the long period of postwar economic expansion and consumer prosperity came to an end, succeeded by slow growth and high inflation

    2. In 1971, for the first time in the twentieth century, the United States experienced a merchandise trade deficit

    3. Nixon took the United States off the gold standard

  B. Stagflation

    1. The United States experienced two oil shocks in the 1970s

    2. By 1973 the United States imported one-third of its oil

    3. America experienced "stagflation"

      a. Misery index

  C. The Beleaguered Social Compact

    1. Faced with declining profits and rising overseas competition, corporations eliminated well-paid manufacturing jobs

      a. The effects on industrial cities were devastating

      b. Growth of cities in the Sun Belt was dramatic

    2. In some manufacturing centers, political and economic leaders welcomed the opportunity to remake their cities as finance, information, and entertainment hubs

    3. Always a junior partner in the Democratic coalition, the labor movement found itself forced onto the defensive

  D. Ford as president

    1. Among his first acts as president, Ford pardoned Nixon

    2. In domestic policy, Ford's presidency lacked significant accomplishment

      a. WIN

    3. The Helsinki Accords were signed in 1975

  E. The Carter Administration

    1. Carter ran for president as an "outsider," making a virtue of the fact that he had never held federal office

    2. Carter had more in common with Progressives of the early twentieth century than more recent liberals

  F. Carter and the Economic Crisis

    1. Carter viewed inflation, not unemployment, as the country's main economic problem

    2. Carter also believed that expanded use of nuclear energy could help reduce dependence on imported oil

      a. Three Mile Island

G. Carter and Human Rights
  1. Carter insisted that foreign policy could not be separated from "questions of justice, equality, and human rights"
  2. Carter's emphasis on pursuing peaceful solutions to international problems and his willingness to think outside the Cold War framework yielded important results
    a. Camp David Accord
    b. Panama Canal
    c. SALT II
  3. Both conservative Cold Warriors and foreign policy "realists" severely criticized Carter's emphasis on human rights
H. The Iran Crisis
  1. The Iranian revolution marked a shift in opposition movements in the Middle East from socialism and Arab nationalism to religious fundamentalism
I. Afghanistan
  1. The president announced the Carter Doctrine in response to the Soviet invasion of Afghanistan

VI. The Rising Tide of Conservatism
A. The Religious Right
  1. The rise of religious fundamentalism during the 1970s expanded conservatism's popular base
  2. Evangelical Christians had become more and more alienated from a culture that seemed to them to trivialize religion and promote immorality
    a. Jerry Falwell and the Moral Majority
B. The ERA Battle
  1. The ERA aroused unexpected protest from those who claimed it would discredit the role of wife and homemaker
    a. To its supporters, the Amendment offered a guarantee of women's freedom in the public sphere
    b. To its foes, freedom for women still resided in the divinely appointed roles of wife and mother
      i. Phyllis Schlafly
C. The Abortion Controversy
  1. Pro-life advocates believed that life begins at conception and abortion is nothing less than murder
  2. Pro-choice advocates believed that a woman's right to control her body includes the right to a safe, legal abortion
  3. The abortion issue drew a bitter, sometimes violent line through American politics
D. The Tax Revolt

       1. Economic anxieties also created a growing constituency for conservative economics

         a. It inspired a critique of government

       2. Economic decline also broadened the constituency receptive to demands for lower taxes

         a. Proposition 13

    E. The Election of 1980

       1. Reagan appealed skillfully to "white backlash"

         a. Emphasized states' rights

       2. Riding a wave of dissatisfaction with the country's condition, Reagan swept into the White House

       3. Jimmy Carter's reputation improved after he left the White House

VII. The Reagan Revolution

    A. Reagan and American Freedom

       1. An excellent public speaker, Reagan's optimism and affability appealed to large numbers of Americans

         a. Reagan made conservatism seem progressive

         b. Freedom became the watchword of the Reagan Revolution

       2. Reagan reshaped the nation's agenda and political language more effectively than any other president since Franklin D. Roosevelt

    B. Reaganomics

       1. Economic freedom for Reagan meant curtailing the power of union, dismantling regulations, and radically reducing taxes

       2. Reagan's tax cuts marked a sharp retreat from the principle of progressivity

       3. "Supply-side economics" assumed that cutting taxes would inspire Americans at all income levels to work harder, since they would keep more of the money they earned

    C. Reagan and Labor

       1. Reagan's firing of striking air traffic controllers inspired many private employers to launch anti-union offensives

       2. "Reaganomics," as critics dubbed the administration's policies, initially produced the most severe recession since the 1930s

    D. The Problem of Inequality

       1. Reagan's policies, rising stock prices, and deindustrialization resulted in a considerable rise in economic inequality

       2. Deindustrialization and the decline of the labor movement had a particularly devastating impact on minority workers

       3. When the national unemployment rate reached 8.9 percent at the end of 1981, the figure for blacks exceeded 20 percent

    E. The Second Gilded Age

       1. In retrospect, the 1980s, like the 1890s, would be widely remembered as a decade of misplaced values

2. Taxpayers footed the bill for some of the consequences
   a. S & L scandal
3. During Reagan's presidency, the national debt rose to $2.7 trillion
F. Conservatives and Reagan
   1. Reagan left intact core elements of the welfare state and did little to advance the social agenda of the Christian Right
G. Reagan and the Cold War
   1. In foreign policy, Reagan breathed new life into the rhetorical division of the world into a free West and unfree East
   2. He proposed an entirely new strategy, the Strategic Defense Initiative
   3. Reagan came into office determined to overturn the "Vietnam syndrome"
   4. Reagan generally relied on military aid rather than American troops to pursue his foreign policy objectives
H. The Iran-Contra Affair
   1. Reagan denied knowledge of the illegal proceedings, but the Iran-Contra affair undermined confidence that he controlled his own administration
I. Reagan and Gorbachev
   1. In his second term, Reagan softened his anticommunist rhetoric and established good relations with Soviet premier Mikhail Gorbachev
      a. *Glasnost* and *perestroika*
J. Reagan's Legacy
   1. Reagan's presidency revealed the contradictions at the heart of modern conservatism
   2. By 1988 "liberal" was a term of political abuse
K. The Election of 1988
   1. The 1988 election seemed to show politics sinking to new lows

## SUGGESTED DISCUSSION QUESTIONS

- What did freedom mean to libertarian conservatives? How did the "new conservatives" define freedom?
- Identify some of the "movements" of the 1960s and describe their progress in the 1970s.
- Discuss the Supreme Court under Warren Burger. Was it a liberal or conservative court? How significant were its major rulings?
- Discuss why conservatives were disappointed with Richard Nixon's domestic policy and with his foreign policy.
- What caused capitalism's "golden age" to end?
- Describe the irony in that President Carter looked like an early-twentieth-century progressive, but yet at the end of his term, the conservative policies associated with Ronald Reagan were already in place.
- How did Ronald Reagan define economic freedom?

## SUPPLEMENTAL WEB AND VISUAL RESOURCES

Détente
*www.cnn.com/SPECIALS/cold.war/episodes/16/*
Part of a series of episodes from the Cold War series produced by CNN,
*Détente* focuses on Nixon's policy to attempt to slow down Cold War
competition.

Watergate
*www.watergate.info/*
This site concentrates on the Watergate scandal that led to the resignation of
President Nixon.

Jimmy Carter
*www.pbs.org/wgbh/amex/carter/*
The "American Experience" series from PBS has a film on the life of Jimmy
Carter. A teachers guide is also available online.

Ronald Reagan
*www.films.com/Films_Home/item.cfm?s=1&bin=7520*
Films for the Humanities and Sciences has the film *The Reagan Legacy*
available for purchase. This BBC production has journalist Charles Wheeler
exploring the legacy of President Ronald Reagan.

Iran-Contra Affair
*www.fas.org/irp/offdocs/walsh/part_i.htm*
The Federation of American Scientists Web site offers a closer look at the
Iran-Contra scandal.

## SUPPLEMENTAL PRINT RESOURCES

Battista, Andrew. "Unions and Cold War Foreign Policy in the 1980s: The
 National Labor Committee, the AFL-CIO, and Central America." *Diplomatic
 History,* 26, no. 3 (2002): 419–52.

Berman, William. *America's Right Turn: From Nixon to Bush.* Baltimore: Johns
 Hopkins University Press, 1994.

Bernardoni, James. *The New Hollywood: What the Movies Did With the
 Freedoms of the Seventies.* Jefferson, NC: McFarland, 2001.

Buckley, William F., Jr., *God and Man at Yale.* Washington, D.C.: Regnery, 1977.

Clymer, Kenton. "Jimmy Carter, Human Rights, and Cambodia." *Diplomatic
 History* 27, no. 2 (2003): 245–78.

Herr, Lois Kathryn. *Women, Power, and AT&T: Winning Rights in the
 Workplace.* Boston: Northeastern University Press, 2003.

Ribuffo, Leo. "Conservativism and American Politics." *The Journal of The
 Historical Society,* 3 no. 2 (2003): 163–75.

Schulzinger, Robert. *Henry Kissinger: Doctor of Diplomacy*. New York: Columbia University Press, 1989.

Shultz, George. *Turmoil and Triumph: My Years As Secretary of State*. New York: Scribner, 1993.

Wicker, Tom. *One of Us: Richard Nixon and the American Dream*. New York: Random House, 1991.

Wilson, William Julius. *The Declining Significance of Race: Blacks and Changing American Institutions*. Chicago: University of Chicago Press, 1978.

## TEST BANK

### Matching

| | | |
|---|---|---|
| g | 1. Milton Friedman | a. first woman appointed on the Supreme Court |
| i | 2. Phyllis Schlafly | b. leader of the Moral Majority |
| f | 3. Henry Kissinger | c. 1964 Republican presidential candidate |
| j | 4. Jimmy Carter | d. Supreme Court chief justice |
| c | 5. Barry Goldwater | e. supporter of the Family Assistance Plan |
| a | 6. Sandra Day O'Connor | f. National Security Advisor |
| d | 7. Warren Burger | g. conservative economist |
| b | 8. Jerry Falwell | h. Strategic Defense Initiative |
| h | 9. Ronald Reagan | i. staunch opponent of the ERA |
| e | 10. Richard Nixon | j. Camp David Accord |


| | | |
|---|---|---|
| h | 1. Church Committee | a. arms for hostages |
| f | 2. The Sharon Statement | b. affirmative action |
| e | 3. Proposition 13 | c. caused by deregulation |
| b | 4. Philadelphia Plan | d. easing of Cold War tensions |
| i | 5. stagflation | e. ban on raising property taxes |
| j | 6. Three Mile Island | f. Young Americans for Freedom |
| d | 7. détente | g. defined freedom as a moral condition |
| g | 8. "new conservatives" | h. investigated the FBI and CIA |
| a | 9. Iran-Contra scandal | i. slow economic growth and high inflation |
| c | 10. savings and loan crisis | j. nuclear power plant accident |

### Multiple Choice

1. Barry Goldwater's 1964 campaign emphasized
    a. increased taxes to pay for the Great Society
    b. an immediate pulling out of Vietnam
  *c. a reduction in governmental regulations

      d. racial equality in the United States

      e. all of the above

2. To "libertarian" conservatives, freedom meant

      a. first and foremost a moral condition

     *b. individual autonomy, limited government, and unregulated capitalism

      c. using government as a vehicle for social reform, ensuring an equal distribution of wealth

      d. what it did in the late eighteenth century—the right to own property and vote

      e. racial equality and the end of a segregated society

3. Many conservative businessmen found intellectual reinforcement in the writings of the economist

      a. John Kenneth Galbraith

     *b. Milton Friedman

      c. Warren Burger

      d. Alan Greenspan

      e. John Maynard Keynes

4. "New conservatives" trusted government to

      a. regulate the economy

     *b. regulate personal behavior

      c. protect civil liberties and the toleration of differences

      d. provide a comprehensive welfare system

      e. all of the above

5. The Port Huron Statement was to the Students for a Democratic Society as the _____ was to the Young Americans for Freedom.

      a. Pentagon Papers

     *b. Sharon Statement

      c. Conscience of a Conservative

      d. Buckley Statement

      e. Church Statement

6. The Environmental Protection Agency, the Occupational Safety and Health Administration, and the National Transportation Safety Board were all established during the administration of which president?

      a. Lyndon Johnson

      b. Gerald Ford

      c. Ronald Reagan

      d. Jimmy Carter

     *e. Richard Nixon

7. Richard Nixon's appointments to the Supreme Court were intended to

      a. continue the liberal trend set by the Warren Court

      b. be balanced with conservatives and liberals

    \*c. lead the court in a conservative direction

    d. break gender barriers by his appointment of the first female justice

    e. appease the Democrats, since he had to work with them in Congress on other issues

8. Expanded freedoms for women in the 1970s were seen through
   a. Title IX, which banned gender discrimination in higher education sports
   b. a higher divorce rate and lower birth rate
   c. the Equal Credit Opportunity Act
   d. more employment opportunities, such as with AT&T
   \*e. all of the above

9. What was not a result of Richard Nixon's 1972 trips to Beijing and Moscow?
   a. The United States and Soviet Union signed an anti–ballistic missile treaty
   b. They brought about increased trade between the United States and China
   \*c. Full diplomatic relations were restored with China
   d. A strategic arms limitation treaty was signed between the United States and Soviet Union
   e. China replaced Taiwan in the United Nations' Security Council

10. What sparked the student antiwar protests at Kent State that resulted in the deaths of four students at the hands of the National Guard?
    a. the election of Richard Nixon
    b. the implementation of the policy called Vietnamization
    c. the Watergate scandal
    d. revelations about the My Lai massacre
    \*e. the escalation of the war into Cambodia

11. What were the burglars at the Watergate apartment complex breaking into when they were arrested?
    a. Daniel Ellsburg's psychiatrist's office
    b. the *Washington Post*'s headquarters
    \*c. the Democratic Party's headquarters
    d. George McGovern's apartment
    e. CREEP's headquarters

12. The Church Committee revealed that since the beginning of the Cold War
    \*a. The CIA and FBI had engaged in abusive actions
    b. The Catholic Church had secretly channeled funds to Third World countries fighting communism
    c. Every administration had traded arms for hostages behind the back of Congress
    d. The Ku Klux Klan had been receiving funds from the FBI to sabotage the Civil Rights movement
    e. The draft process had unfairly drafted the poor and minorities, while white, middle-class men were often exempt

13. What caused the American economy to slip in the 1970s?
    a. spending on Vietnam
    b. oil embargoes
    c. the shift away from manufacturing
    d. spending on the Great Society
    *e. all of the above

14. The centerpiece of Jimmy Carter's foreign policy was
    a. détente
    *b. human rights
    c. military strength
    d. Strategic Defense Initiative
    e. the CIA

15. In response to the Soviet invasion of Afghanistan, President Carter
    a. boycotted the Berlin Olympics
    *b. placed an embargo on grain exports to the Soviet Union
    c. withdrew the SALT I treaty from the Senate for ratification
    d. decreased military spending
    e. all of the above

16. The opponents of the ERA defined freedom for women
    a. within the public sphere
    b. as the right to control their own bodies
    *c. as residing in the roles of wife and mother
    d. as economic opportunity
    e. as the right to an easy divorce

17. The election of 1980 reflected
    a. the end of conservatism
    b. the validation of big government
    c. a return to progressivism
    *d. growing frustration over America's condition
    e. a referendum for the ERA

18. The 1980s could easily be called the Second
    *a. Gilded Age
    b. Progressive Era
    c. Era of Good Feelings
    d. New Deal Society
    e. Industrial Revolution

19. Ronald Reagan's economic policy focused on
    *a. tax cuts
    b. high tariffs
    c. government spending on welfare

    d. empowering unions

    e. increasing government regulations on industry

20. By the end of Reagan's second term in office, he viewed the Soviet Union

    a. as an "evil empire"

    b. with great disdain

    c. as an expansionist power

    d. as a strong ally

    *e. with much less suspicion

## True or False

T    1. Milton Friedman argued that government should seek to regulate neither the economy nor individual conduct.

F    2. Libertarians and the "new conservatives" each defined freedom the same way.

F    3. The student organization Young Americans for Freedom's manifesto was called the Port Huron Statement.

T    4. Despite being a Republican, while in office President Richard Nixon expanded the welfare state.

F    5. Richard Nixon put forth the Philadelphia Plan, which supported affirmative action, and was bitterly disappointed when the Supreme Court ruled that it was unconstitutional.

F    6. Despite efforts by the Supreme Court, the South's public schools were still more segregated by 1990 than the North's.

T    7. Before the 1970s, the American Psychiatric Association listed homosexuality as a psychiatric disorder.

T    8. Richard Nixon and Henry Kissinger had an unconventional approach to the Cold War through the policy of détente, which lessened tensions between the United States and the Soviet Union.

F    9. The Church Committee investigated the Watergate break-in, concluding that Richard Nixon had ordered the White House cover-up.

T    10. In 1971, for the first time in the twentieth century, the United States experienced a merchandise trade deficit.

T    11. By 1973 the United States imported one-third of its oil supply.

T    12. Neither President Gerald Ford nor Vice-President Nelson Rockefeller had been elected to their offices.

F    13. Immediately after the end of the Vietnam War, Ford issued an unconditional pardon to all of the draft dodgers.

F    14. As a Washington insider who had served three terms in the Senate, Jimmy Carter was well educated in domestic and foreign policies before becoming president.

F    15. In spite of the efforts of conservatives like Phyllis Schlafly, the Equal Rights Amendment was passed by Congress and ratified by enough states.

T    16. Ronald Reagan was a New Deal Democrat and union leader before switching parties and running for governor of California.

F    17. Reagan's presidency was successful in large part because of his close, hands-on governing style that oversaw every detail.

T    18. Under Reagan's tax policy, the highest tax rate fell from 70 percent to 28 percent.

T    19. Economic freedom for Reagan meant curtailing the power of unions, dismantling regulations, and radically reducing taxes.

F    20. Like fellow Republican Teddy Roosevelt did in 1902 during the coal strike, Ronald Reagan supported striking air traffic controllers and forced the FAA into mediation.

## Short Answer

*Identify and give the historical significance of each of the following terms, events, and people in a paragraph or two.*

1. Reaganomics
2. ERA
3. Warren Court
4. stagflation
5. Barry Goldwater
6. affirmative action
7. Libertarian versus "new conservatives"
8. Watergate
9. détente
10. Moral Majority

## Essay Questions

1. Journalist Theodore White commented that both the conservatives and liberals used the term "freedom" as the foundation of their platforms. Both groups demanded either "Freedom Now" or "Freedom for All." Analyze how both groups were using "freedom." What meaning did they give to the word? Be sure to emphasize both the similarities and differences in each group's approach to the term "freedom."

2. The conservative movement was not a cohesive movement. Explain the positions taken by libertarians versus the "new conservatives." How did each understand the meaning of freedom?

3. Thinking back to the previous chapter, compare the New Left's student manifesto, the Port Huron Statement, with that of the Young Americans for Freedom manifesto, the Sharon Statement. How does each address the problems of American society in the 1960s? How does each invoke the meaning of freedom?

4. Was Richard Nixon a good conservative? Why, or why not?

5. Explain why that although liberals celebrated the fall of Richard Nixon, in fact the public revulsion against Watergate undermined the foundations of liberalism itself.

6. The 1970s was the only decade besides the 1930s in the twentieth century that Americans on average were poorer at the end of the decade than when it began. Compare the economic crisis of the 1970s with the 1930s. What were the causes of each? How did the government respond to each? How was labor affected in each decade? What eventually turned the economy around in each case?

7. Eric Foner suggests that President Jimmy Carter had more in common with the Progressives of the early twentieth century than with more recent liberals. Thinking back to Chapter 18, discuss what Progressive characteristics Carter demonstrated. Would he have been a successful Progressive presidential candidate in the early 1900s? Why, or why not?

8. Analyze the debate over the Equal Rights Amendment. Who was for it and who was against it? How did each side define freedom for women? What does the debate tell us about American society in the 1970s?

9. Ultimately, how conservative was Ronald Reagan's tenure in office? Why might some conservatives feel he did not go far enough, while some liberals felt that he dismantled too much?

10. Analyze the success of Reagan's administration in both domestic and foreign policy. Explain why he left office popular with the public, despite leaving behind him an enormous national debt.

11. Compare how successful the women's movement and the civil rights movement were by the end of 1988. What achievements had been made? What methods did each movement employ to best affect? Which was more successful, and why? Did each group achieve its desired "freedoms"?

## CHAPTER 27

# Globalization and Its Discontents, 1989–2000

This chapter concentrates on the Clinton years. Opening with the 1999 anti-globalization demonstrations held in Seattle protesting the World Trade Organization, the chapter explores the challenges that the twenty-first century faces in balancing globalization, economic justice, and freedom. Highlighting this challenge is the "Declaration for Global Democracy" in *Voices of Freedom*. The chapter then looks at the end of the Cold War and the Bush administration. Having an opportunity to remake the world immediately after the fall of communism, George Bush spoke of a New World Order, committed American troops in Panama, and organized a coalition to fight Iraq in the Gulf War. Unable to sustain his popularity after that war in face of an economic recession, Bush lost the 1992 election to Bill Clinton. Like Carter, Clinton tried to elevate human rights in international policy. At home he practiced triangulation, adopting some moderate Republican issues, while rejecting the more contentious ones. Despite Clinton's series of scandals, he left office in 2001 with a high approval rating. The contested election of 2000 illustrated how divided American society was at the turn of the century. While many Americans benefited from the economic boom of the 1990s, divisions within society still remained, which are seen through the "culture wars." The chapter concludes with a summary of facts about American society in 2000.

## CHAPTER OUTLINE

I. The Battle of Seattle and Antiglobalization

II. The Post–Cold War World
   A. The Crisis of Communism
      1. Tiananmen Square freedom demonstration in 1989 ended in violence
      2. Germany reunified in 1990
         i. Velvet Revolution

3. By December 1991, the Soviet Union ceased to exist
4. The end of the Cold War ushered in a truly worldwide capitalist system
B. A New World Order?
1. Although George Bush talked of a New World Order, no one knew what its characteristics would be
C. The Gulf War
1. Bush intervened when Iraqi dictator Saddam Hussein invaded Kuwait in 1990
2. The Gulf War was the first post–Cold War international crisis
3. Bush identified the Gulf War as the first step in the struggle to create a world based on democracy and global free trade
D. The Election of Clinton
1. The economy slipped into recession in 1991 and Bill Clinton took advantage to win the election
a. A charismatic campaigner, Clinton conveyed sincere concern for voters' economic anxieties
2. A third candidate, the eccentric Texas billionaire Ross Perot, also entered the fray
E. Clinton in Office
1. In his first two years in office, Clinton turned away from some of the social and economic policies of the Reagan and Bush years
2. Clinton shared his predecessor's passion for free trade
a. NAFTA
F. The Health Care Debacle
1. The major policy initiative of Clinton's first term was a plan to address the rising cost of health care and the increasing number of Americans who lacked health insurance
a. The plan would have provided universal coverage though large groupings of organization like the HMOs
b. Attacked by doctors, health insurance companies, and drug companies, the plan was not implemented
G. The "Freedom Revolution"
1. In 1994, for the first time since the 1950s, Republicans won control of both Houses of Congress
a. Newt Gingrich and the Contract with America
2. Viewing their electoral triumph as an endorsement of the Contract, Republicans moved swiftly to implement its provisions
H. Triangulation
1. Clinton rebuilt his popularity by campaigning against a radical Congress
2. Clinton signed into law a Republican bill that abolished the program of Aid to Families with Dependent Children (AFDC)
3. "Triangulation" meant that Clinton embraced the most popular Republican policies like welfare reform, while leaving his opponents with extreme positions such as hostility to abortion rights and

environmental protection, unpopular among suburban middle-class voters

4. Clinton easily defeated Republican Bob Dole in the presidential contest of 1996, becoming the first Democrat elected to two terms since FDR

I. Clinton and World Affairs

1. Clinton took steps to encourage the settlement of long-standing international conflicts, and tried to elevate support for human rights to a central place in international relations

2. The Oslo Agreement brought temporary peace between Israel and Palestine

3. Like Carter, Clinton found it difficult to balance concern for human rights with strategic and economic interests
   a. Rwanda
   b. Haiti

J. The Balkan Crisis

1. The most complex foreign policy crisis of the Clinton years arose from the disintegration of Yugoslavia

2. With the Cold War over, protection of human rights in the Balkans gave NATO a new purpose

K. Human Rights

1. Human rights emerged as a justification for interventions in matters once considered the internal affairs of sovereign nations

III. A New Economy?

A. The Computer Revolution

1. Computers and the Internet produced a "new economy"

2. Microchips made possible the development of entirely new consumer products

3. The computer transformed American life

4. The Internet expanded the flow of information and communications more radically than any invention since the printing press

B. Global Economic Problems

1. American economic expansion in the 1990s seemed all the more remarkable since other advanced countries found themselves bogged down in difficulty

2. Many Third World countries faced large trade deficits and problems repaying loans from foreign banks and other institutions

C. The Stock Market Boom and Bust

1. In the United States, economic growth and talk of a new economy sparked a frenzied boom in the stock market reminiscent of the 1920s

2. Investors were especially attracted to the new "dot-coms"—companies that conducted business via the Internet and seemed to symbolize the promise of the new economy

      3. The bubble burst on April 14, 2000, when stocks suffered their largest one-day drop in history

  D. The Enron Syndrome

      1. Only after the market dropped did it become apparent that the stock boom of the 1990s had been fueled in part by fraud

        a. Enron

  E. Fruits of Deregulation

      1. The sectors of the economy most affected by the scandals—energy, telecommunications, and stock trading—had all been subjects of deregulation

  F. Rising Inequality

      1. The boom that began in 1995 benefited nearly all Americans

        a. However, overall, in the last two decades of the twentieth century, the poor and middle class became worse off while the rich became significantly richer

      2. The economy, in large part due to NAFTA, continued its shift away from manufacturers

      3. High-tech firms did not create enough high-paying jobs to compensate

      4. In 2000, well over half the labor force worked for less than $14 per hour, a wage on which families found it very difficult to make ends meet

IV. Culture Wars

  A. The Newest Immigrants

      1. Because of shifts in immigration, cultural and racial diversity became increasingly visible in the United States

      2. As in the past, most immigrants became urban residents

      3. Post-1965 immigration formed part of the worldwide uprooting of labor arising from globalization

      4. For the first time in American history, women made up the majority of newcomers

  B. The New Diversity

      1. Latinos formed the largest single immigrant group

      2. Numbering over 35 million at the turn of the century, Latinos nearly equaled blacks and were poised to become the largest minority group in the United States

      3. Only after 1965 did immigration from Asia assume large proportions

  C. Multiculturalism

      1. "Multiculturalism" became the term for a new awareness of the diversity of American society

  D. African-Americans in the 1990s

      1. Most African-Americans remained in a more precarious situation than whites or many recent immigrants

E. The Courts and Race
  1. The justices made it increasingly difficult for victims of discrimination to win lawsuits and proved increasingly sympathetic to the pleas of whites that affirmative action plans discriminated against them
  2. Despite the nation's growing racial diversity, school segregation was on the rise
F. The Spread of Imprisonment
  1. Blacks, compared to other Americans, had an extremely high rate of imprisonment
  2. As the prison population grew, a "prison-industrial complex" emerged
    a. Convict labor
G. The Burden of Imprisonment
  1. Over one-quarter of all black men could expect to serve time in prison at some time during their lives
  2. Blacks were also more likely than whites to suffer execution
  3. The continuing frustration of urban blacks exploded in 1992
    a. Rodney King
H. The Continuing Rights Revolution
  1. In 1990, newly organized disabled Americans won passage of the Americans with Disabilities Act
  2. The campaign for gay rights continued to gain momentum in the 1990s
    a. AIDS
I. The Identity Debate
  1. Conservatives, and some traditional liberals as well, decried "identity politics" and multiculturalism for undermining a common sense of nationhood
  2. Increased cultural diversity and changes in educational policy inspired harsh debates
  3. For a time, nativism gained renewed respectability
    a. *The Bell Curve*
    b. *Alien Nation*
J. Cultural Conservatism
  1. The culture wars were battles over moral values that raged throughout the 1990s
    a. Pat Robertson and the Christian Coalition
  2. It sometimes appeared during the 1990s that the country was refighting old battles between traditional religion and modern secular culture
K. "Family Values" in Retreat
  1. The census of 2000 showed "family values" increasingly in disarray
  2. *Casey v. Planned Parenthood of Pennsylvania* repudiated the centuries-old doctrine that a husband has a legal claim to control the body of his wife

L. The Anti-Government Extreme
   1. At the radical fringe of conservatism, the belief that the federal government posed a threat to American freedom led to the creation of private militias who armed themselves to fend off oppressive authority
      a. Gun ownership
   2. An Oklahoma federal building was bombed by Timothy McVeigh in 1995

V. Impeachment and the Election of 2000
   A. The Impeachment of Clinton
      1. In the 1980s and 1990s scrutiny of politicians' private lives became far more intense than in the past
      2. From the day he took office, Clinton was challenged by charges of misconduct
         a. Whitewater
         b. Paula Jones
         c. Monica Lewinsky
   B. The Disputed Election
      1. The 2000 election was between Al Gore and George W. Bush
      2. The election proved to be one of the closest in the nation's history
         a. Florida
      3. As in 1877, it fell to Supreme Court justices to decide the outcome
   C. The 2000 Result
      1. The most remarkable thing about the election of 2000 was not so much its controversial ending as the even division of the country it revealed
      2. Democrats blamed the Supreme Court, Ralph Nader, and sheer bad luck for Bush's narrow victory
   D. A Challenged Democracy
      1. Coming at the end of the "decade of democracy," the 2000 election revealed troubling features of the American political system at the end of the twentieth century
      2. Evidence abounded in 2000 of a broad disengagement from public life

VI. Freedom and the New Century
   1. Worldwide life expectancy in the twentieth century rose from 40 to 67 years, and the literacy rate from 25 percent to 80 percent
   2. In the United States, people lived longer and healthier lives in 2000 compared to previous generations, and enjoyed a level of material comfort unimagined a century before
   3. In 2000, nearly one American in seven was older than 65
   4. Freedom remained a crucial point of self-definition for individuals and society at large

## SUGGESTED DISCUSSION QUESTIONS

- What events between 1989 and 1991 encouraged the spread of globalization, and how?
- Why did George Bush intervene in the Middle East in 1990–91? What freedoms was he defending?
- How did computers change American life? Compare the impact of the computer with the impact of the automobile in the 1920s.
- Discuss what caused the economy boom of the 1990s and who did and did not benefit from it.
- Discuss the Supreme Court in the 1990s. Was it conservative? Liberal?
- Discuss the culture wars. Who was on each side of the debate? How did each side use freedom?
- Compare the experiences of Latinos with Asian-Americans in the late twentieth century.

## SUPPLEMENTAL WEB AND VISUAL RESOURCES

The Gulf War
*www.pbs.org/wgbh/pages/frontline/gulf/*
PBS's *Frontline* documentary on the Gulf War is available on this site. It includes a chronology, maps, and transcripts from the broadcast.

The 2000 Election
*www.cnn.com/ELECTION/2000/*
This CNN site has an archive of information pertaining to the controversial election of 2000.

Impeachment Trial for Clinton
*www.pbs.org/newshour/impeachment/*
This PBS site provides information that enables a detailed understanding of the impeachment trial of Bill Clinton.

NAFTA
*www.hartford-hwp.com/archives/40/index-b.html*
This site has a history of the NAFTA agreement with different perspectives.

Clinton Sex Scandal
*www.films.com/Films_Home/item.cfm?s=1&bin=9220*
This site has a film available for purchase pertaining to the Clinton scandal with Monica Lewinsky.

## SUPPLEMENTAL PRINT RESOURCES

Brock, David. *Blinded By the Right: The Conscience of an Ex-Conservative.* New York: Three Rivers Press, 2003.

Klein, Joe. *The Natural: The Misunderstood Presidency of Bill Clinton.* New York: Broadway Books, 2003.

Pitti, Stephen. *The Devil in Silicon Valley: Northern California, Race, and Mexican Americans.* Princeton, NJ: Princeton University Press, 2003.

Powell, Colin. *My American Journey.* New York: Ballantine, 1996.

Schlesinger, Arthur, Jr. *The Disunitng of America: Reflections on a Multicultural Society.* New York: W. W. Norton & Company, 1998.

Stephanopoulos, George. *All Too Human: A Political Education.* Boston: Back Bay, 2000.

Takaki, Ronald. *A Different Mirror: A History of Multicultural America.* Boston: Little, Brown & Company, 1994.

## TEST BANK

### Matching

| | | |
|---|---|---|
| d | 1. Ralph Nader | a. Contract with America |
| g | 2. Pat Robertson | b. Panama dictator |
| h | 3. Ross Perot | c. Supreme Court justice |
| f | 4. Bill Clinton | d. Green Party |
| b | 5. Manuel Noriega | e. attorney general |
| i | 6. Hillary Clinton | f. triangulation |
| j | 7. Saddam Hussein | g. Christian Coalition |
| a | 8. Newt Gingrich | h. 1992 independent presidential candidate |
| e | 9. Janet Reno | i. health care |
| c | 10. Ruth Bader Ginsburg | j. Iraqi dictator |

| | | |
|---|---|---|
| i | 1. EITC | a. Israel and Palestinian agreement |
| e | 2. Freedom Revolution | b. dismantled by Clinton |
| g | 3. Operation Desert Storm | c. awareness of American diversity |
| a | 4. Oslo Accords | d. free-trade zone |
| j | 5. Velvet Revolution | e. 1994 mid-term election |
| h | 6. Tiananmen Square | f. largest corporate employer in 2000 |
| d | 7. NAFTA | g. Kuwaiti freedom |
| c | 8. multiculturalism | h. Chinese demonstration for democracy |
| b | 9. welfare | i. cash payment for low-income workers |
| f | 10. Wal-Mart | j. fall of communism in Eastern Europe |

### Multiple Choice

1. What was said to be the concept of the 1990s?
    a. liberty
    b. money

    c. technology
*d. globalization
    e. liberalism

2. The internationalization of commerce and culture and the reshuffling of the world's peoples have been going on for only the last _____ years.
    a. 50
    b. 100
    c. 200
    d. 400
*e. 500

3. The Velvet Revolution was
*a. the collapse of communism in eastern Europe
    b. the Republican victory in the 1994 congressional elections
    c. the end of apartheid in South Africa
    d. the mass organization of middle-class black men in Washington, D.C.
    e. what Democrats called Bill Clinton's victory in 1992

4. George Bush immediately sent American troops where after Saddam Hussein invaded Kuwait?
    a. Israel
*b. Saudi Arabia
    c. Kuwait
    d. Iran
    e. Egypt

5. Who did Clinton appoint to head the panel on health care reform?
    a. Ruth Bader Ginsberg
    b. Janet Reno
*c. Hillary Clinton
    d. Phyllis Schlafly
    e. Sandra Day O'Connor

6. The Freedom Revolution was
    a. the collapse of communism in eastern Europe
*b. the Republican victory in the 1994 congressional elections
    c. the end of apartheid in South Africa
    d. the mass organization of middle-class black men in Washington, D.C.
    e. what Democrats called Bill Clinton's victory in 1992

7. What did Clinton end?
    a. the Cold War
    b. food stamps
    c. public housing
*d. welfare
    e. all of the above

8. Bill Clinton's foreign policy centered on
   *a. elevating human rights to a central place in international relations
   b. defeating the few pockets of communism left in the world
   c. taking a hard line against economic competitors like Mexico and Canada
   d. building what he called a New World Order
   e. preemptive strikes to weed out dictatorial leaders that posed a threat to American security

9. What spurred the "new economy"?
   a. automobiles
   b. housing
   c. NAFTA
   d. televisions
   *e. computers

10. By 2000, unemployment in America stood at about _____ percent.
    a. 15
    b. 12
    c. 8
    *d. 4
    e. 2

11. The sectors of the economy that were most affected by the scandals of the late 1990s and early twenty-first century had all been
    a. run by Democrats who gave large campaign donations to Bill Clinton
    b. victims of harsh financial policies put forth during the Reagan administration
    *c. subjects of deregulation
    d. dot-com industries
    e. bailed out during the savings and loan crisis

12. By 2000, approximately _____ Muslims lived in the United States.
    a. 100,000
    b. 500,000
    c. 1 million
    d. 2 million
    *e. 3 million

13. Which ethnic group's average family income in 2000 surpassed that of whites?
    *a. Asians
    b. Muslims
    c. Latinos
    d. blacks
    e. Indians

14. The battles that raged throughout the 1990s over moral values were called
    a. conservative wars
    *b. culture wars
    c. Christian wars
    d. Supreme Court wars
    e. family value wars

15. *Casey v. Planned Parenthood of Pennsylvania*
    a. upheld the view that those who used violence against abortion clinics had to be prosecuted to the fullest extent of the law
    b. ruled that a woman had to inform her husband before getting an abortion
    c. overturned *Roe v. Wade*
    *d. repudiated the centuries-old claim that a husband had a legal claim to control the body of his wife
    e. was a triumph for supporters of the pro-life position

16. What city witnessed riots and looting in 1992 after tensions snapped over an episode of policemen beating an unarmed black man?
    a. New York
    b. San Francisco
    c. Chicago
    *d. Los Angeles
    e. Houston

17. The 1995 truck bombing of the federal building in Okalahoma City was organized by
    a. militant black separatists
    b. a left-wing paramilitary group
    *c. a far-right private militia group
    d. Islamic fundamentalists
    e. Osama bin Laden

18. Which of the following was a scandal of the Clinton Administration?
    a. Teapot Dome
    *b. Whitewater
    c. Watergate
    d. Whiskey Ring
    e. Iran-Contra

19. *Bush v. Gore* ordered
    a. that victory be given to Bush
    b. the recount in Florida to finish within one week
    c. Florida to vote again in a separate election
    *d. Florida to halt its recount
    e. that Florida replace all of its balloting machines

20. Which was not a demand of the Global Exchange outlined in its "Declaration for Global Democracy"?
    a. Globalization could not continue without representation from all sectors of society
    b. Global trade and investment must be instruments for achieving equitable and sustainable development
    c. The WTO as presently constructed had to be replaced
    d. Global trade agreements must not undermine the ability of each nation state or local community to meet its citizens' needs
    *e. Globalization had to continue along a course set by corporate leaders as they best understood the needs of consumers

## True or False

F   1. The Velvet Revolution was horribly bloody and cost the lives of hundreds of thousands of Europeans.

T   2. The first countries to declare independence from the Soviet Union were the Baltic states.

T   3. Bush identified the Gulf War as the first step in the struggle to create a world based on democracy and global free trade.

F   4. Ross Perot challenged Bill Clinton for the Democratic presidential nomination.

F   5. Bill Clinton won the support of labor in proposing NAFTA.

F   6. In concert with past liberal Democrats, Clinton worked hard to balance the federal budget.

F   7. Doctors, health insurance companies, and drug companies supported the comprehensive health care plan that was presented by the Clinton administration.

T   8. Winning reelection in 1996, Clinton became the first Democrat elected to two terms since FDR.

T   9. Human rights emerged as a justification for interventions in matters once considered the internal affairs of sovereign nations during the Clinton years.

T   10. Investors in the "new economy" were especially attracted to the new dot-coms—companies that conducted business via the Internet and seemed to symbolize the promise of the new economy.

T   11. In 2000, well over half the labor force worked for less than $14 per hour, a wage on which families found it very difficult to make ends meet.

F    12. The largest corporate employer in America in 2000 was Microsoft.

F    13. Books like *The Bell Curve* renewed the liberal passions for reform, calling upon government to further provide for the working class.

T    14. At the radical fringe of conservatism, the belief that the federal government posed a threat to American freedom led to the creation of private militias who armed themselves to fend off oppressive authority.

F    15. Asians, compared to other Americans, had an extremely high rate of imprisonment by the end of the century as illegal immigration accelerated.

F    16. By the end of the century, school desegregation in America was complete, with high schools across the country enjoying interracial student bodies.

T    17. A convict might answer a call placed to TWA (Trans World Airlines), as convict labor was on the rise by the end of the century.

T    18. Democrats blamed the Supreme Court, Ralph Nader, and sheer bad luck for George W. Bush's narrow victory in 2000.

T    19. By 2000, women were receiving more than half of all the college degrees awarded in the United States.

F    20. "No globalization without representation" was the rallying cry of congressional Republicans.

## Short Answer

*Identify and give the historical significance of each of the following terms, events, and people in a paragraph or two.*

1. World Trade Organization
2. Balkans
3. culture wars
4. immigration
5. triangulation
6. Hillary Clinton
7. NAFTA
8. *The Bell Curve*
9. "new economy"
10. Velvet Revolution

## Essay Questions

1. Analyze how and why the most pressing concern for the twenty-first century is the relationship among globalization, economic justice, and freedom.

2. Explain how the Gulf War was the first step in the struggle to create a world based on democracy and global free trade.

3. Thinking back to previous chapters, explain how Clinton accomplished for Reaganism what Eisenhower had done for the New Deal, and Nixon for the Great Society.

4. Compare the stock market boom of the 1990s with that of the 1920s. What fueled the markets in each decade? Who participated in the market in each decade? Why did each market's proverbial bubble burst?

5. In the 1970s, the U.S. economy began to shift away from manufacturers. The trend continued into the 1990s. Explain why this was so and who was affected by this shift. What were the benefits and consequences of this shift?

6. Thinking back to previous chapters, explain how the culture wars of the 1990s caused Americans to rethink the definition of American nationality just as the Alien Act, Irish immigration of the antebellum era, and the "new immigrants" of the turn of the century had done in the past.

7. Analyze how cultural conservatives defined freedom. What arguments did they make in defense of freedom? How valid were their arguments?

8. Evaluate the "rights revolution" that began in the 1950s. Your essay ought to chronicle the various Supreme Court decisions and legislation that enlarged the rights of various Americans. How successful was this revolution by 2000?

## CHAPTER 28

# Epilogue: September 11 and the Next American Century

This chapter concentrates on the recent events of September 11 and the Iraqi war. The chapter opens by recalling the terrorist attack on America. Before September 11 the Bush administration practiced a conservative agenda, cutting taxes, building defenses, and dismantling environmental policies. After the attacks, Bush launched a war on terror, and quickly identified an "axis of evil," which he dealt with in part through Operation Iraqi Freedom. American foreign policy was fundamentally altered with the 2002 National Security Strategy that advocated preemptive war. The document defined national security in terms of defending freedom and an excerpt is highlighted in *Voices of Freedom*. The war on terrorism affected society at home with the USA PATRIOT Act and a failing economy. Finally, the chapter looks at two monumental Supreme Court decisions, which reflected that the "rights revolution" was here to stay.

## CHAPTER OUTLINE

I. Terrorist attacks on September 11, 2001

II. The War on Terrorism
   A. Bush before September 11
      1. Bush had proven himself an effective proponent of what he called "compassionate conservatism"
      2. He won a narrow victory, but pursued a strongly conservative agenda
         a. Tax cut
         b. Environmental policies
   B. Bush and the World
      1. Bush emphasized American freedom of action, unrestrained by international treaties and institutions
      2. The Bush administration announced that it would not abide by the Kyoto Treaty of 1997

C. "They Hate Freedom"
    1. An outpouring of popular patriotism followed the September 11 attacks
    2. The Bush administration benefited from this patriotism and identification with government
    3. Bush told America that "freedom and fear are at war"
D. Enduring Freedom
    1. The Bush Doctrine immediately emerged
       a. War in Afghanistan
E. The Axis of Evil
    1. Remarkable changes in American foreign policy quickly followed the Afghan war
    2. In 2002, Bush identified Iraq, Iran, and North Korea as an "axis of evil"
F. The National Security Strategy
    1. The National Security Strategy outlined a fundamental shift in American foreign policy
       a. Defense of freedom
       b. Relied on a large military
       c. Advocated "preemptive" war
    2. Relations between the United States and Europe were on a "collision course"
G. An American Empire?
    1. Charges quickly arose that the United States was bent on establishing itself as a new global empire
    2. In America, the term "empire" was used positively
H. The Iraq War
    1. The Bush administration in 2002 announced a goal of "regime change" in Iraq
    2. The decision split the Western alliance and inspired a massive antiwar movement throughout the world
I. The Iraq War
    1. Operation Iraqi Freedom's purpose was to "defend our freedom" and "bring freedom to others"
    2. Rarely in its history had the United States found itself so isolated from world public opinion
    3. For the third time in less than a century the United States had embarked on a crusade to create a new world order

III. The Aftermath of September 11 at Home
  A. Security and Liberty
    1. Congress rushed to pass the USA PATRIOT Act
       a. Conferred unprecedented powers on law-enforcement agencies
    2. In November 2001, the Bush administration issued an executive order authorizing the holding of secret military tribunals for noncitizens deemed to have assisted terrorism

    a. "Enemy combatants"

    b. "TIPs"

B. The Jobless Recovery

    1. During 2001, the economy slipped into a recession

    2. For the first time since the 1980s, the average pay at all income levels, from top to bottom, failed to keep up with inflation

    3. Racial minorities suffered the most from the economy's continued shedding of jobs in the early 2000s

    4. The combination of a faltering economy, increased military spending, and the 2001 tax cuts produced a rapid rise in budget deficits at both the national and state levels

C. The Constitution and Liberty

    1. Two significant Supreme Court decisions in June 2003 revealed how the largely conservative justices had come to accept that the social revolution that began during the 1960s could not be undone

      a. Affirmative action

      b. Homosexuality

D. Learning from History

    1. It is still far too soon to assess the full impact of September 11 on American life

    2. As in the past, freedom is central to Americans' sense of themselves as individuals and as a nation

## SUGGESTED DISCUSSION QUESTIONS

- How did the terrorist attacks of September 11 differ from other terrorist attacks in the United States?
- Debate whether or not the Bush Doctrine was successful.
- Ask the students to compare the World War I experience of the German-Americans and the World War II experience of Japanese-Americans to the September 11 experience of Muslim-Americans.
- Does the USA PATRIOT Act violate civil liberties? Why or why not?
- Is America an empire? Is that a good or a bad thing?
- What do the 2003 Supreme Court decisions say about how permanent the "rights revolution" is?

## SUPPLEMENTAL WEB AND VISUAL RESOURCES

USA PATRIOT Act

*www.epic.org/privacy/terrorism/hr3162.html*

This site contains the full USA PATRIOT Act document as well as archives of material pertaining to the Act.

September 11
*www.ssrc.org/sept11/*
This Social Science Research Council–sponsored site contains numerous essays relating to September 11

Inside the Terror Network
*www.pbs.org/wgbh/pages/frontline/shows/network/*
This PBS *Frontline* video offers a look into the terror network that orchestrated September 11

## SUPPLEMENTAL PRINT RESOURCES

Albright, Madeleine. "Bridges, Bombs, or Bluster?" *Foreign Affairs* 82, no. 5 (2003): 2–19.

Begala, Paul. *It's Still the Economy, Stupid: George W. Bush, The GOP's CEO.* New York: Simon & Schuster, 2002.

Friedman, Thomas. *Longitudes and Attitudes: Exploring the World After 9/11.* New York: Anchor, 2003.

Longley, Clifford. *Chosen People: The Big Idea That Shaped England and America.* London: Hodder & Stoughton, 2002.

Rahe, Paul A., et. al. "11 September: A Symposium." *The Journal of The Historical Society* 2, no. 2 (2002): 145–214.

## TEST BANK

### Matching

| | | |
|---|---|---|
| f | 1. axis of evil | a. global warming |
| d | 2. Al Qaeda | b. compassionate conservative |
| a | 3. Kyoto Treaty | c. attorney general |
| b | 4. George W. Bush | d. terrorist group |
| c | 5. John Ashcroft | e. Afghanistan |
| e | 6. Taliban | f. Iran, Iraq, North Korea |

### Multiple Choice

1. The Bush administration
   a. broke the 1972 ABM treaty
   b. rejected the Kyoto Treaty
   c. opposed the establishment of an International Criminal Court
   d. enacted a large tax cut
   *e. all of the above

2. Operation Enduring Freedom
    a. was a war against the Iraqi dictator Saddam Hussein
    b. was successful in capturing Osama bin Laden in its first week
    c. dismantled the nuclear weapons program of North Korea
    *d. was an all-out war on terrorism
    e. was fought primarily in Iran

3. What made Bush's 2002 National Security Strategy fundamentally different from previous American policy?
    a. It began by defining freedom
    b. It called for a huge military buildup
    c. It did not refrain from nuclear weapons
    *d. It advocated the use of preemptive war
    e. It called for multilateral action

4. The USA PATRIOT Act
    a. overhauled airport security measures
    *b. expanded law enforcement agencies to conduct secret searches and detain suspected aliens
    c. required every American to swear a loyalty oath
    d. ceased all Islamic immigration into the United States
    e. was vetoed by George W. Bush for violating civil liberties, but overridden by Congress

5. Two landmark Supreme Court cases ruled in 2003 dealt with
    a. homosexuality and abortion
    b. affirmative action and disabled persons
    *c. homosexuality and affirmative action
    d. abortion and affirmative action
    e. disabled persons and homosexuality

## True or False

F      1. Palestinian militants who were retaliating against American support for Israel orchestrated the attacks of September 11.

T      2. George W. Bush called himself a "compassionate conservative."

T      3. George W. Bush emphasized American freedom of action, unrestrained by international treaties and institution.

F      4. The war in Iraq was widely supported by the global community as seen through the widespread rallies of support, especially in Europe.

T      5. The Iraq war marked the third time in less than a century that the United States embarked on a crusade to create a new world order.

F      6. The USA PATRIOT Act is a remarkably short and concise document.

F    7. Despite strong opposition from the ACLU, the TIPs program continued.

T    8. The combination of a faltering economy, increased military spending, and the 2001 tax cuts produced a rapid rise in budget deficits at both the national and state levels by 2003.

T    9. Black unemployment rates were double that for whites in 2003.

F   10. *Lawrence v. Texas* upheld affirmative action.

## Short Answer

*Identify and give the historical significance of each of the following terms, events, and people in a paragraph or two.*

1. USA PATRIOT Act
2. Bush Doctrine
3. axis of evil
4. affirmative action
5. *Lawrence v. Texas*
6. Department of Homeland Security
7. John Ashcroft
8. "compassionate conservatism"

## Essay Questions

1. Fully discuss and examine the limitations placed upon freedom after September 11. Then compare those circumstances with those during both the McCarthy era and World War I. What is the balance between security and freedom during war? Does the Constitution protect citizens' rights during wartime? Should dissent be equated with lack of patriotism? Why, or why not?

2. Looking back to the early Cold War period, compare the National Security Strategy of George W. Bush in *Voices of Freedom* with that of NSC-68. How did each outline fundamental shifts in American foreign policy? How did each define freedom?

3. Evaluate whether or not the United States is an empire today. Be sure to discuss why some believe that it is and why others disagree.

4. Reflect back on the last half century and comment upon the Langston Hughes poem that concludes the chapter. What is the poem's meaning? If Hughes were alive today, do you think he would argue that his poem is still relevant? Why, or why not?